HEAVEN
and
Beyond

Knowing
the reality of
your hope.

By Dave Weeks

Heaven and Beyond will take each reader down a biblical path that has been undiscovered by most Christians. This journey will be amazing, joyful, and endearing. Your appreciation for what life in Jesus Christ is, will be enriched each step of the way. Knowing the reality of your hope will make it worth it all. God's eternal kingdom is unveiled with Jesus Christ presenting His Father's mansions to all those named in the Lamb's book of like. Come and see!

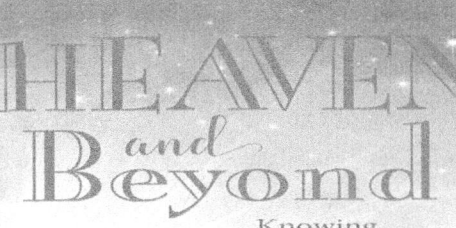

Knowing the reality of your hope.

By Dave Weeks

By

DAVE WEEKS

© 2019

PUBLICATIONS

Baptist World Cult Evangelism

P.O. Box 352

Jefferson, GA 30549-0352

www.bwce.org

All quotations of Scripture are taken from the Authorized King James Version.

HEAVEN AND BEYOND

© 2019 Baptist World Cult Evangelism

P.O. Box 352, Jefferson, GA 30549-0352

Printed by Facing the Facts, Jefferson, GA

Cover by Addyman Design

Printed in the United States of America

Library of Congress Control Number: 2019901974

Weeks, Dave

Heaven and Beyond / by Dave Weeks.

p.cm.

Includes bibliographical reference.

ISBN 9781796827958 (Paperback)

1. HEAVEN — AFTERLIFE. 2. ESCHATOLOGY— STUDY OF THE LAST DAYS. 3. CHRISTIAN LIVING — DOCTRINE.

FOREWORD

Dave Weeks, the Author of *Checkmate* ... and *The Sunday School Book* (TSSB), has done it again! In the same dynamic manner as he approaches his ministry to the cults. Brother Weeks has penned yet another scholarly publication, *Heaven and Beyond — Knowing the reality of your hope.*

The premise of this work is that the Bible plainly teaches us that believers will live on the new earth after the old earth is destroyed (2 Peter 3:13). There is no specific Scripture which speaks of an eternal third heaven, for God Himself will dwell in the holy city. To argue otherwise is to do so based on the silence (absence) of Scripture, or the presumption that Scripture about the third heaven at this present time automatically applies to the eternal state, or is the result of enthusiastic "off-the-cuff" preaching and comments by favorite preachers or teachers whom we admire and enjoy, or is in our subconscious due to stirring gospel music on the subject of heaven. (Don't trash your song books. Just be careful what you sing!) One composer commented that he did not care who wrote the laws of his nation as long as he could write the music. Why? Music is an extremely powerful influence. Therefore, it is always wise to check our lyrics against the Word of God.

One final test of any Bible position, application, or emphasis is the fruit of that teaching. Proclaiming the truth that living for Jesus and faithfully serving Him here and now will, in fact, enhance our kingdom position later is certain to ratchet up our positive motivation for godly behavior in these last days. Of course, our primary motivation is always to please and glorify the Lord Jesus Christ in everything we do. As always, Brother Weeks writes with simplicity so that any layperson of any age can understand and apply the truth. May I say… "Thank you, Brother Dave, for challenging us to Kingdom Living." I am…

Your Friend,

Dr. Brad Weniger, Pastor

Central Baptist Church

Woodbridge, Virginia

COMMENTS FROM A FRIEND

You are about to begin a journey of heavenly proportions. Dave Weeks does a great job of laying out the importance of the gospel of God's kingdom and the reality of our eternal hope. With scriptural support and contextual clarity, this book communicates from start to finish what the Bible says about *Heaven and Beyond*. You will be challenged to think beyond heaven and look to eternity.

What a joy it is to know that your name can be written in the Lamb's book of Life and God the Father is fulfilling His kingdom promise that our Lord and Saviour, Jesus Christ taught us in the model prayer, "Thy Kingdom come thy will be done on earth as it is in heaven." (Matthew 6:9-13). To God be the glory.

Dr. Shane Roberson, Sr. Pastor

Maysville Baptist Church

Maysville, Georgia

DEDICATION

This may be the last one of my publications and it is my greatest joy to dedicated it to the High and Lofty One that inhabits eternity. The One who heals the brokenhearted and tells the number of the stars and calls them all by their names. To the One who takes pleasure in them that fear Him, which in an honest and good heart, having heard the word, keep it, and bring forth fruit with patience. To the One who holds the reality of my hope in His eternal kingdom and has kept me ever in His presence. He is the One-Triune God existing eternally in three persons: God the Father, God the Son, and God the Holy Spirit. He created all things for His honor and glory. It is because of Him alone that I have the blessed privilege to write of His promise to make all things new.

INTRODUCTION

Heaven and Beyond — Knowing the reality of your hope is a text that focuses on God's eternal kingdom of righteousness, which begins in Revelation 21. It takes the reader from Genesis 1:1, where God created this present earth, to Revelation 21:1, where God creates a new heaven and a new earth.

Gen 1:1

In the beginning God created the heaven and the earth.

Rev 21:1

And I saw a new heaven and a new earth: for the first heaven and the first earth were passed away; and there was no more sea.

In the periods of time between these two events, the deceased saints of God have been in different places.

Luke 16:22-23

22 And it came to pass, that the beggar died [Lazarus], and was carried by the angels into Abraham's bosom: the rich man also died, and was buried;

23 And in hell he lift up his eyes, being in torments,

and seeth Abraham afar off, and Lazarus in his bosom.

Luke 23:43

And Jesus said unto him [the repentant malefactor], Verily I say unto thee, To day shalt thou be with me in paradise.

When Jesus led the captivity captive, the deceased saints went to the third heaven where He sits at the right hand of the Father.

Matt 27:52

And the graves were opened; and many bodies of the saints which slept arose.

Eph 4:8

Wherefore he saith, When he ascended up on high, he led captivity captive, and gave gifts unto men.

When the rapture of the church occurs, saints will be taken up by Jesus to the third heaven to be with Him.

1Thess 4:15-17

15 For this we say unto you by the word of the Lord, that we which are alive and remain unto the coming of the Lord shall not prevent them which are asleep.

16 For the Lord himself shall descend from heaven

with a shout, with the voice of the archangel, and with the trump of God: and <u>the dead in Christ shall rise first:</u> 17 Then <u>we which are alive and remain shall be caught up together with them in the clouds, to meet the Lord in the air: and so shall we ever be with the Lord</u>. During the millennium, saints will return with Christ to this earth and reign with Him for 1000 years.

2Tim 2:12

<u>If we suffer, we shall also reign with him:</u> if we deny him, he also will deny us:

Rev 20:6

Blessed and holy is he that hath part in the first resurrection: on such the second death hath no power, but they shall be priests of God and of Christ, and shall <u>reign with him a thousand years.</u>

At this point, I would like to give you a quote that was made by a leading Baptist theologian in the early 1900's. His name is Lewis Sperry Chafer. He was the founder and first president of Dallas Theological Seminary (DTS). The title of his publication is *Major Bible Themes* and the first edition was printed in 1926 and published by DTS. The revised edition was copyrighted in 1974 by DTS and printed by Zondervan Publishing House, Grand Rapids, Michigan. In the third paragraph on page 373, the writer's comments are a review of Revelation 21 and the beginning of Revelation 22. Here is what he said, "Considering the fact that the new heavens and the new earth will be the eternal abode of the saints, it is remarkable that there is comparatively little description of it in the entire Scripture."

It is important to understand, since that book was written, there has been a major shift from this doctrinal position. One of the reasons for that change is the songs in our hymn books. For centuries, the church has been singing songs about the new Jerusalem, the holy city as being the home of the church. Because the repetition of music is more prone to shape one's thinking than Bible doctrine, the church continues to believe what it sings about the holy city. The result is that the musical lyrics have taken precedence over biblical truth and people don't know it.

What I would like to do now is to give you a way to determine if this shift in doctrine agrees with the context of Scripture. If you have read the back page of this book, you have seen our comments about the Berean principle. It is requoted below. I have added here a second way of describing this principle to show you how it functions. The Berean principle is an inside look at the Scriptures for answers and understanding of God's Word. This inside look is done without the influence from commentaries and "camp positions." Now, what follows is the quote from the back page. "What makes this book different than perhaps any of the other heaven books? It's the "Berean principle." What is the Berean principle? It is the sourcing method (like a bibliography list in the back of most books) that supports the authority of the author's publication. The only source that the Bereans used was God. They had other options of course, like we do, but they chose only the Scriptures. Let's take a look at Acts 17:10-11: *And the brethren immediately sent away Paul and Silas by night unto Berea: who coming thither went into the synagogue of the Jews. 11 These [Bereans] were more noble than those in Thessalonica, in that they received the word with all readiness of mind, and searched the scriptures daily, whether those things were so."*

At different times, people have asked me why there are so many different interpretations of the Bible. The answer is very simple. It is because not everyone who believes in God and who reads the Bible use <u>the same rules</u> to interpret what they read. There are rules of interpretation. When these rules are followed, they act as a referee who, <u>without any bias</u>, makes the same ruling in every like situation. Without these rules, one can make the Bible say whatever he wants it to say.

Rightly dividing the word of truth requires an understanding of the rules that enables one to do that. One's knowledge of these rules must be a working knowledge as opposed to a general knowledge. A good example of this would be an automobile mechanic who knows how to connect the spark plug wires to their right position in the ignition. A general knowledge, by contrast, would be a person who simply knows that the spark plug wires are connected to the ignition. What's missing is that he doesn't know the firing order; he does not know that spark plug one connects to ignition position four. If the spark plug wires are not connected to the right position in the ignition, the engine will not crank.

Once a person has a working knowledge of <u>the rules, they are useless unless one is committed to applying them</u>, especially when they show a conflict with his present belief.

If you agree to these rules and apply them correctly and honestly, there is no truth in a verse, a chapter, a book, or in all of Scripture that cannot be rightly divided.

If you ignore these rules and follow the camps and commentaries, then you will find yourself, one day, to be the least in God's kingdom.

Matthew 5:19

Whosoever therefore shall break one of these least commandments, and shall teach men so, he shall be called the least in the kingdom of heaven: but whosoever shall do and teach them, the same shall be called great in the kingdom of heaven.

2Timothy 2:15, by any means, is not one of the least of God's commandments. To those in ministry, it is one of the most demanding.

Of these four rules, the first two are the most important. They require no theological degrees, just observation, thorough searching, and honesty. God knows your heart and He will help anyone who truly wants to know the truth. Learning how to recognize the truth involves studying the rules that enable one to rightly divide it. Are you willing to do that? Great, let's get started.

1. Context Rule – The applicable meaning of words, or paragraphs, or chapters, or books of the Bible is taken from the circumstances and conditions that surround it. The contexts reveal the writer's true thoughts.

2. Harmony Rule – A truth that is God-given will always be in harmony with the whole of God's Word. For example, consider Genesis 3:21: *Unto Adam also and to his wife did the LORD God make coats of skins, and clothed them.* The harmony rule is the second most important rule because it highlights all contradictions

to any previous truth that has been established.

3. Grammar Rule – Every verse of Scripture must be interpreted in agreement with or in terms of its grammatical structure. The grammar rule is the third most important rule because it determines, controls, and limits the interpretation syntactically. Syntax is the branch of linguistics that deals with the application of set rules in a language.

4. Language Rule – This is the awareness of how language is being used in the verse (i.e., literal, figurative, or symbolic language and the grammatical functions that apply to each part of speech). In John 8:58, Jesus said, *Before Abraham was, I am.* This statement is literal; Jesus existed before Abraham. In John 10:9, He says, *I am the door* .... This statement is figurative; it is a metaphor. And in Revelation 8:6, we read, *And the seven angels which had the seven trumpets prepared themselves to sound.* This statement is symbolic; the trumpet is a symbol for judgment.

Now, let's put these rules into play like you would in a game of chess. In chess, the king rule is that it can only move one space at a time. If your opponent moves the king five spaces, when placed in check, one could never win. Let's take that same scenario and apply it to this question about where the dwelling place of the saints will be in the new earth of Revelation 21. The two views are:

1 Saints inherit the new earth — position one person

2 Saints inherit the new Jerusalem which they call heaven — position two person

If you would hear someone take his proof text from Philippians 3:20 and Revelation 21:1 to prove position two, what should you do?

Php 3:20

For our conversation is in <u>heaven</u>; from whence also we look for the Saviour, the Lord Jesus Christ.

Position two people make heaven, in the above verse, the new Jerusalem in Revelation 21 instead of the third heaven where Jesus is now.

The first thing that you need to know is there are three heavens mentioned in Scripture. They are our immediate atmospheric heaven, the stellar heaven, (containing the sun, moon, and stars), and the third heaven, the home of God and the current dwelling place of the saints. In Philippians 3:20, Paul and the saints are looking for Jesus to come and rapture the church. With these facts at hand, we can evaluate the two positions and find the truth.

When a position two person reads Phil 3:20, he says that heaven is the holy city, the new Jerusalem. And then, all the people in his congregation say, Amen, except the one who knew and saw that his explanation violated the context and harmony rules. Where were these rules violated? Can you show us? Yes!

Heaven, in the Philippians verse, is the third heaven where Jesus is now. How do you know that? The Apostle Paul and the saints are looking for Jesus to come at the rapture (1Thess 4:13-17). This is when Jesus leaves the third heaven, where He is now, and comes for His church. The fact that Jesus is in the third heaven and will come from there, and not the new Jerusalem, is how one knows that the number two position is false. The context is misrepresented by saying the third heaven is the new Jerusalem in Revelation 21.

Heaven in Revelation 21:1 is the new atmospheric heaven. How do you know that? It comes from the context. Take a look:

Rev 21:1 And I saw a new heaven and a new earth: for the first heaven [atmospheric heaven] and the first earth [our present earth] were passed away; and there was no more sea.

The first heaven was the atmospheric heaven and the first earth was land. In the new earth, earth is also land and the new heaven is that new earth's new atmospheric heaven.

The Harmony rule also comes into play here. The position that heaven, in Revelation 21:1, is the holy city, the new Jerusalem, contradicts a number of other verses that read like these:

Psa 37:11

But the meek [the meek represents all the saints] shall inherit the earth; and shall delight themselves in the abundance of peace.

Jesus even quoted this verse here in Matt 5:5, *Blessed are the meek: for they shall inherit the earth.*

The golden rule of interpretation is said to be that when the plain sense makes common sense, seek no other sense. We all have that sense; we just need to ask the Lord to help us to use it when reading His Word.

You can learn more about how the Lord used the tool of hermeneutics by reading His dialog with Satan in Matthew 4:1-10. Hope this has been a help.

What you will find to be contextually true is that the new Jerusalem is not *heaven*. The new Jerusalem is not called heaven; it is called *the holy city*. The atmospheric heaven is the only place called heaven in the eternal state. After Revelation 21, the third heaven will no longer exist, for God's eternal dwelling place will be in the holy city. The eternal occupants of the new Jerusalem are His servants who have suffered and died for their faith and faithfulness. The rest of the saints will dwell on the new earth and go in and out of the holy city to praise and worship God and the Lamb. May the true reality of your hope, be your hope!

Contents

GETTING STARTED

This book is about an Awesome God and the mysteries of His eternal kingdom of righteousness. It begins immediately after this present earth is completely destroyed. Then God creates a new heaven and a new earth and makes all things new. The children of the kingdom will dwell there for time without end. This was the gospel of the kingdom of God that Jesus and His disciples preached. It is the reality of every believer's hope. Yes, there is a better day coming!

Each of the main chapters has a kingdom connection and begins to unveil these glorious mysteries. The book of Genesis tells us of the creation of the present heaven and earth. In Revelation 21, He ends His message by telling us of the future creation of a new heaven, a new earth, and a new Jerusalem. The climax of it all is in an eternal state of perfection. This glorious state of being begins with Christ's eternal kingdom of righteousness. There He promises to end death, sin, suffering, sorrow, and there will be no more pain.

My passion for writing this text has been building steadily for a number of years. The reality of the believer's hope seems to have disappeared. The lines of musical lyrics have replaced the lines of Scripture. More and more one reads and hears from numerous sources that all who are saved will spend eternity in heaven. This troubled me greatly. So, I began looking for reasons as to why this was happening. The answer was simple — the message of Christ's gospel of His eternal kingdom of righteousness is no longer taught or preached. Very seldom is it heard in any gospel message, in hymns, or Christian literature. Understanding the reality of one's eternal hope is linked to Christ's repeated teachings about the coming kingdom of righteousness. He told His disciples that the kingdom of God was a mystery that would now be revealed. He first mentioned this in the parable of the sower — Luke 8:10 *And he said, Unto you it is given to know the <u>mysteries of the kingdom of God</u>: but to others in parables; that seeing they might not see, and hearing they might not understand.*

Some of what you are about to read now is repeated from the introduction. The reason it appears again is that sometimes people skip introductions. The points that are being stressed are important. So, I ask for your patience if you are reading this for a second time.

One of the first doctrinal books that I purchased, as a new believer, was written by Lewis Sperry Chafer. He was the founder and first president of Dallas Theological Seminary (DTS). Inside the cover I wrote "June 5, 1975," which was the date that I purchased it. The title is *Major Bible Themes* and the first edition was printed in 1926 and published by DTS. My revised edition was copyrighted in 1974 by DTS and printed by Zondervan Publishing House, Grand Rapids, Michigan. In the third paragraph on page 373, the writer's comments are a review of Revelation 21 and the beginning of Revelation 22. Here is what he said, "Considering the fact that the new heavens and the new earth will be the eternal abode of the saints, it is remarkable that there is comparatively little description of it in the entire Scripture."

After reviewing this, I called four of the major universities or schools that Baptist and Bible churches are currently using and asked to talk with the professor of eschatology. My findings were both positive and negative. The positive point was that none of these colleges taught or were teaching that heaven is the eternal abode of the saints. Now, the negative point is most interesting. One of the professors stated that when he begins teaching on this subject his students are bewildered. They act as though they never heard this before — beyond heaven (the third heaven, the place where saints go when they die) is Christ's eternal kingdom of righteousness. The gospel of the kingdom of God is something completely new. Here, take a look for yourself! Rev 21:1 *And I saw a new heaven* [atmospherical heaven] *and a new earth* [physical earth]*: for the first heaven and the first earth were passed away; and there was no more sea.*

Let's talk about heaven for a moment. Which heaven do you mean? I mean the heaven where Jesus is now. To clear up some confusion about heaven, it is a good time to identify the three heavens spoken of in Scripture. First of all, there is the atmospheric heaven where the birds fly in the sky above us. Genesis 1:20 speaks of it: *And God said, Let the waters bring forth abundantly the moving creature that hath life, and fowl that may fly above the earth in the open firmament of heaven.* Second, there is the stellar heaven which is the starry heaven. It is what David spoke of in Psalms 8:3-4: *When I consider thy heavens, the work of thy fingers, the moon and the stars, which thou hast ordained; 4 What is man, that thou art mindful of him? and the son of man, that thou visitest him?* The third heaven is mentioned in Psa 11:4: *The LORD is in his holy temple, the LORD'S throne is in heaven.* Paul spoke of it here, 2Cor 12:2,4: *I knew a man in Christ above fourteen years ago, (whether in the body, I cannot tell; or whether out of the body, I cannot tell: God knoweth;) such an one caught up to the third heaven. 4 How that he was caught up into paradise, and heard unspeakable words, which it is not lawful for a man to utter.* And Eph 4:10: *He that descended is the same also that*

29

ascended up far above all heavens [the third heaven], *that he might fill all things.*

Every child of God should know the reality of this hope in Jesus Christ. The gospel that Jesus preached is where that reality lies. In that message, He brought hope to a world trapped in sin, death, and judgment.

It is my joy that you have chosen *Heaven and Beyond.* Might the sweet Lord Jesus give you an understanding that will lead you to His eternal kingdom. May He open the windows of heaven with His words and invite you to visit your new home where all things will become new.

The Berean Principle

Be ready always! 1 Pet 3:15

Rightly dividing truth! 2 Tim 2:15

Acts 17:11
"... they received the word with all <u>readiness</u> of mind, and searched the scriptures daily, whether those things were so."

GETTING INTRIGUED

For about six-thousand years now people have lived and died on this earth. God has woven into Scripture a beautiful picture of how the curse of death will vanish. The first thread of this promise is found here:

Gen 3:15

And I will put enmity between <u>thee</u> [... that old serpent, which is the Devil, and Satan (Rev 20:2)] and the woman, and between thy seed and her seed; it shall bruise thy head, and thou shalt bruise his heel.

The next thread is woven into the garment of the sacrifice:

Gen 3:21:

Unto Adam also and to his wife did the LORD God make coats of skins [most likely a lamb], and clothed them.

The third thread is seen in Adam and Eve's first two sons:

Gen 4:3-5:

3 And in process of time it came to pass, that Cain

brought of the fruit of the ground an offering unto the LORD.

4 And Abel, he also brought of the firstlings of his flock and of the fat thereof. And the LORD had respect unto Abel and to his offering [because it was a type representing Jesus Christ, the Lamb of God]:

5 But unto Cain and to his offering he had not respect. And Cain was very wroth, and his countenance fell.

This began the long line of types and rituals that would lead to Jesus Christ, the sinless Lamb of God. It was He alone who would be the final sacrifice. By His blood, we would be cleansed from our sins and become children of God and children of His kingdom.

It is important for us to understand the two people groups that are mentioned in Gen 3:15, i.e., the seed of the devil (the children of the devil, the wicked) and the seed of the woman (the righteous, the saints). These two groups are mentioned continuously throughout the Bible. You are either in one or the other. That's it!

In Psalms One there is a breakdown of the wicked into two subgroups. They are seen again in the New

Testament (NT). Let's take a look:

Psa 1:5-6

5 Therefore the ungodly shall not stand in the judgment, nor sinners in the congregation of the righteous.

6 For the LORD knoweth the way of the righteous: but the way of the ungodly shall perish.

People are divided into two main groups. They are the ungodly and the righteous. The wicked are divided into these two subgroups — the ungodly and the sinners in the congregation of the righteous. The first subgroup describes the wicked who are not "church people" (the ungodly) and the second subgroup describes the wicked who are in the church (sinners in the congregation of the righteous). Jesus taught His disciples this reality in both the parable of the sower and the parable of the wheat and the tares. This stands as somewhat of an eyeopener as to why there have always been conflicts and divisions in the congregation of the righteous.

Here is a list of some of these two groups that are

contrasted with one another: ungodly and godly; sons of man and sons of God; wicked and righteous; child of the devil and child of God; lost and saved; tares and wheat; children of the wicked one, children of the kingdom; goats and sheep; the fool and the wise, just to mention a few. It is also very important to identify these two groups accurately by their context when they appear. The failure to do this can and has resulted in many misinterpretations of frequently quoted passages like this one:

Rom 3:10-12

10 As it is written, There is none righteous, no, not one:

11 There is none that understandeth, there is none that seeketh after God.

12 They are all gone out of the way, they are together become unprofitable; there is none that doeth good, no, not one.

Did you ever take the time to locate the Old Testament (OT) references where Paul quoted these verses from and determine which people group they represent? Let's take a look at:

Rom 3:10-12 and Ps 14:1-4; 53:1-4:

10 As it is written, There is none righteous, no, not one:

11 There is none that understandeth, there is none that seeketh after God.

12 They are all gone out of the way, they are together become unprofitable; there is none that doeth good, no, not one [the "none" people spoken of here are the wicked, the seed of Satan and Cain].

Psa 14:1-4:

1 The <u>fool</u> [the wicked] hath said in his heart, There is no God. They are corrupt, they have done abominable works, there is none that doeth good.

2 The LORD looked down from heaven upon the <u>children of men,</u> [here a reference to the wicked] to see if there were any that did understand, and seek God.

3 They are all gone aside, they are all together become filthy: there is none that doeth good, no, not one.

4 Have all the <u>workers of iniquity</u> [these are the wicked] no knowledge? who eat up <u>my people</u> [these are the righteous] as they eat bread, and call not upon the LORD.

35

Psalms 10 is an excellent example of the unrepentant heart of the wicked and their hatred for God and how they follow the way of Cain straight into perdition. Here are two of the many verses in Psalms 10 that describe the wicked:

Psa 10:4-5

4 The wicked, through the pride of his countenance, will not seek after God: God is not in all his thoughts. 5 His ways are always grievous; thy judgments are far above out of his sight: as for all his enemies, he puffeth at them.

Perhaps one of the best examples of these two groups of sinners can be seen at Calvary. Jesus was crucified between two sinners (all have sinned). One was wicked and had an unrepentant and wicked heart, the other was sinful and had a repentant heart.

Knowing that there are only two people groups throughout all of Scripture and rightly identifying them is one of the most important steps to understanding the climax in the last chapters of the book of Revelation. Now that we have laid this foundation, the next two chapters will build upward from here. It's going to be an exciting journey, I promise you.

John's thoughts must have flooded his heart with joy as he penned the final book of the Bible. He had seen Jerusalem completely destroyed. There was not one stone upon another that was not thrown down. Israel was gone. Those who survived were scattered. Great persecution was leveled upon Christians. Yet, John saw the kingdom of God that was promised to him by Jesus during His transfiguration. He was about to see the glorious climax of it all and, just in that moment, he sees first what you are about to read next:

Rev 21:1

And I saw a new heaven and a new earth: for the first heaven and the first earth were passed away; and there was no more sea.

I wonder how many times people have read this verse and never paused to ponder the significance of these last three words, *no more sea.* To get some idea of what this means, think of the Pacific Ocean. It is the largest of the five oceans of the world. If you would take all the continents on the earth, you could put them all into the basin of the Pacific Ocean.

God put *no more sea* there to spike our anticipation about our eternal destiny. A destiny that places the children of God in Christ's eternal kingdom of righteousness.

The gospel of the kingdom of God was the message that Jesus preached. It excited the people. It was a kingdom for who-so-ever-will, not just the Jews. In the last verses in Acts 28:30-31, Paul was preaching the same message, *30 And Paul dwelt two whole years in his own hired house, and received all that came in unto him, 31 Preaching the kingdom of God, and teaching those things which concern the Lord Jesus Christ, with all confidence, no man forbidding him.*

This gospel of God's kingdom has all but disappeared in our generation and perhaps even much longer than that. The result is that people no longer know the reality of their hope. Some people know that when they die, they will be in heaven. Beyond that, most of them don't have a clue. There is much to learn about the kingdom of God. Knowing these truths will enrich your expectations about the future and replace the darkness of death with the light of God's kingdom. Keep looking up, saints!

The Berean Principle

Be ready always! 1 Pet 3:15

Rightly dividing truth! 2 Tim 2:15

Acts 17:11
"... they received the word with all <u>readiness</u> of mind, and searched the scriptures daily, whether those things were so."
© BWCE

KINGDOM BEGINNING

It might be best to start with a definition of a kingdom. A kingdom requires two elements: a person who is king (the ruler) and people who are his subjects (those who occupy his domain). In every kingdom there is rank and file. This describes a hierarchy in which people or groups are ranked one above the other according to status or authority.

Now it may be helpful to further introduce this subject with a question that stimulates your thinking. This question will help to lay the foundation that will support the framework that follows a little later. Here's the question: "Is it true that, before God created anything in Genesis 1:1, He alone existed?" From the standpoint of Scripture, it is a forgone conclusion that the answer to this question is yes. Here's why:

Isa 43:10 "Ye are my witnesses, saith the LORD, and my servant whom I have chosen: that ye may know and believe me, and understand that I am he: <u>before me there was no God formed, neither shall there be after</u>

me."

Isa 44:24 "Thus saith the LORD, thy redeemer, and he that formed thee from the womb, I am the LORD that maketh all things; that stretcheth forth the heavens alone; that spreadeth abroad the earth by myself."

The account in Genesis tells us that God created everything in six literal days. As a part of His creation work, He also created all of the heavenly creatures, but when they were created, during those six days, He did not mention. God's act of creating heaven and earth is what gives us a starting point for His kingdoms. In His earthly kingdom, man was the highest being created and was given dominion and authority to rule in His behalf. In God's heavenly kingdom, Lucifer is believed to have had the same dominion and authority. So, it can be said that from the beginning of time, God created two kingdoms, one on earth and the other in heaven. As Genesis Chapter Three unfolds, it reveals Lucifer's plot to gain dominion of earth and replace Adam. All the rest is history.

In Genesis Chapter Four, the enmity between Satan's

seed (the wicked) and the seed of the woman (the righteous) begins. It begins with Cain and Able. This enmity continues until the end of Revelation 20, when Satan is cast into the lake of fire with all those who have rejected Jesus Christ as the Eternal Son of God. After this, there will only be one kingdom composed of those who are named in the Lamb's book of life. This will begin God's eternal kingdom of righteousness.

Some people suffer from the delusion that Satan is the one who has control of this world. Let all those who entertain such thoughts be assured that God alone has control of this planet and all of its creation. Many Scriptures assure us of this truth and here is one of them in Psalms 24:1: *The earth is the LORD'S, and the fulness thereof; the world, and they that dwell therein.*

When Satan offered Jesus all the kingdoms of the world in Matthew 4:8-9, he was lying — they weren't his to offer, for the Creator alone is that Sovereign King: *8 Again, the devil taketh him up into an exceeding high mountain, and sheweth him all the kingdoms of the world, and the glory of them; 9 And saith unto him, All these things will I give thee, if thou wilt fall down and worship me.*

When Pilate asked Jesus if He were the king of the Jews, Jesus said yes, and not only is He king of the Jews, but He is King of kings and Lord of lords: Revelation 19:16:

And he hath on his vesture and on his thigh a name written, KING OF KINGS, AND LORD OF LORDS.

YOU SHOULD REMEMBER THIS

Before creation in Genesis 1:1 only God existed.

From the beginning of creation, the kingdom of God existed in two places: in heaven and on earth.

God did not mention during the six days of creation when He created the heavenly kingdom.

There are only two groups of people in the world: the righteous and the wicked (Gen 3:15).

Teach others what you learn — they will love it.

KINGDOM HISTORY

Scripture provides a captivating history of how God unveils the promise of His eternal kingdom. Selecting the word "kingdom" in my Bible app resulted in 321 references. The purpose for this search was to find the verses that would be pointing to the Revelation 21 kingdom climax. Remember, this is how the more noble Bereans did their studies without commentaries. Context and harmony are always the rules that referee and review each of our "plays" — the interpretation of Scripture. God has given our generation a completed Bible and some of the best tools ever developed to study His Word. Take your seats in the stands and watch perhaps the most fascinating play of words which chronicle His kingdom that you may have ever seen.

God was not taken by surprise at any event that occurred at any time. Before the fall of the earthly and heavenly kingdoms, God's subjects had the privilege of His presence. He walked with Adam and Eve in the garden and the heavenly creatures were before His throne. After sin entered both kingdoms, that changed. God is so awesome that He had the beginning and the end in sight before creation.

In the mind of God, the Lamb was already slain before the world was ever created as mentioned in Rev. 13:8, right? *And all that dwell upon the earth shall worship him* [the Lamb, the Messiah, Jesus], *whose names are not written in the book of life of the Lamb slain from the foundation of the world.* The existence of Jesus before the world is also clearly stated in John 17:5: A*nd now, O Father, glorify thou me with thine own self with the glory which I had with thee before the world was.* One could also say, without contradiction, that the body of Jesus, which would be nailed to the cross, also existed in the mind of God before the world existed. If you take this thought and link it with the creation of man in Gen 1:26, you have a greater understanding of the harmony of our likeness to Jesus in creation: *And God said, Let us make man in our image, after our likeness:* [the body of Jesus that would be nailed to the cross] *and let them have dominion over the fish of the sea, and over the fowl of the air, and over the cattle, and over all the earth, and over every creeping thing that creepeth upon the earth.* We also know that in the climax, Rev 21, once again we will have a body like Jesus' body in 1John 3:2: *Beloved, now are we the sons of God, and it doth not yet appear what we shall be: but we know that, when he shall appear, we shall be like him; for we shall see him as he is.* This is one of the main aspects of the reality of our hope. Hallelujah, praise the Lamb!

One of the first references to the "forever kingdom" or the kingdom of righteousness has its thread in this passage in 1Sam 13:13: *And Samuel said to Saul, Thou hast done foolishly: thou hast not kept the commandment of the LORD thy God, which he commanded thee: for now would the LORD have established thy kingdom upon Israel for ever.* Because of Saul's disobedience, he forfeited the privilege of having the royal lineage. God knew of a man who was after His own heart. That person was David, the lowly shepherd boy. When his father's sheep were in danger, he showed great courage by facing a lion and a bear to protect them, and the Lord was his strength. David went on to show his heart for his God by standing up to Goliath. He asked a question, "Is there not a cause?" The honor of David's Heavenly Father was being defamed by the enemies of Israel and in faith he put his life on the line to give Him glory. Although David yielded to the desires of his flesh with Bathsheba and suffered the consequences, yet his Lord would give him this link to the eternal kingdom in 2Sam 7:16: *And thine house* [David's] *and thy kingdom shall be established for ever before thee: thy throne shall be established for ever.* David's seed would be forever linked to Christ's eternal kingdom of righteousness that begins in Revelation 21.

In the chronicle of this everlasting kingdom, the scepter (the emblem of absolute power) of righteousness divided the last kingdom from all other kingdoms, including the millennial reign of Christ. Why is that true? It is true because during Christ's 1000-year reign, there will be sin, death, and rebellion. The next two references connect the dots to the eternal kingdom in Psalms 45:6: *Thy throne, O God, is for ever and ever: the sceptre of thy kingdom is a right sceptre.* And in Hebrews 1:8: *But unto the Son he saith, Thy throne, O God, is for ever and ever: a sceptre of righteousness is the sceptre of thy kingdom.*

The rest of these eternal kingdom references show how our awesome God linked them throughout the pages of the Old Testament. As you are viewing them, just think of how privileged our generation is to have them all in view with one search command of a smart phone.

Isa 9:6-7

6 For unto us a child is born, unto us a son is given: and the government shall be upon his shoulder: and his name shall be called Wonderful, Counsellor, The mighty God, The everlasting Father, The Prince of Peace.

7 Of the increase of his government and peace there shall be no end, upon the throne of David, and upon his kingdom, to order it, and to establish it with judgment

and with justice from henceforth even <u>for ever</u>. The zeal of the LORD of hosts will perform this.

Isa 65:17

For, behold, I create <u>new heavens and a new earth</u>: and the former shall not be remembered, nor come into mind.

Isa 66:22

For as the <u>new heavens and the new earth</u>, which I will make, shall remain before me, saith the LORD, so shall your seed and your name remain.

Dan 2:44

And in the days of these kings shall the God of heaven set up <u>a kingdom, which shall never be destroyed</u>: and the kingdom shall not be left to other people, but it shall break in pieces and consume all these kingdoms, and <u>it shall stand for ever.</u>

Dan 7:13-14

13 I saw in the night visions, and, behold, one like the Son of man came with the clouds of heaven, and came to the Ancient of days, and they brought him near before him.

14 And there was given him dominion, and glory, and a kingdom, that all people, nations, and languages, should serve him: his dominion is an <u>everlasting dominion</u>, which shall not pass away, and <u>his kingdom that which shall not be destroyed</u>.

Dan 7:27

And the kingdom and dominion, and the greatness of the kingdom under the whole heaven, shall be given to the people of the saints of the most High, whose kingdom is an <u>everlasting kingdom</u>, and all dominions shall serve and obey him.

To leave these verses in 2Peter 3 out of this great chronicle would be amiss. May the sweet Lord Jesus speak to each of our hearts and might we feel His longing for them to be fulfilled.

2Pe 3:9-14

9 The Lord is not slack concerning his promise, as some men count slackness; but is longsuffering to us-ward, <u>not willing that any should perish</u>, but that all should come to repentance.

10 But the day of the Lord <u>will come as a thief in the</u>

night; in the which the <u>heavens shall pass away</u> with a great noise, and the elements shall melt with fervent heat, the earth also and the works that are therein shall be burned up.

11 Seeing then that all these things shall be dissolved, what manner of persons ought ye to be in all holy conversation and godliness,

12 Looking for and hasting unto the coming of the day of God, wherein the heavens being on fire shall be dissolved, and the elements shall melt with fervent heat?

13 Nevertheless we, according to his promise, look for <u>new heavens and a new earth, wherein dwelleth righteousness.</u>

14 Wherefore, beloved, seeing that <u>ye look for such things</u>, be diligent that ye may be found of him in peace, without spot, and blameless.

KINGDOM MESSAGE

Mark 1:14-15

14 Now after that John was put in prison, Jesus came into Galilee, preaching the gospel of the kingdom of God, 15 And saying, The time is fulfilled, and the kingdom of God is at hand: repent ye, and believe the gospel.

The kingdom message was the good news about the kingdom of God, His eternal kingdom of everlasting righteousness. How long should the gospel of the kingdom of God be preached? Jesus said until the end spoken of in these verses in Matthew and Revelation: Matt 24:14: *And this gospel of the kingdom shall be preached in all the world for a witness unto all nations; and then shall the end come.* Rev 14:6-7: *And I saw another angel fly in the midst of heaven, having the everlasting gospel to preach unto them that dwell on the earth, and to every nation, and kindred, and tongue, and people.*

This may turn out to be one of the most encouraging

subjects that you have studied in a long time. You can be assured that it will be a chapter with a bent page or a book marker for repeated references in the future. Perhaps you will see the gospel with the dots connected in the way the Author revealed it. If it's possible for the good news to get better, it may happen now.

In staying with the Berean search principle, here is the most common definitions of the gospel.

gospel = a message concerning Christ, salvation, and the good news of the kingdom of God, each of the first four books of the New Testament, a thing that is absolutely true

The good news of the kingdom might be stated as the absolute truth about <u>where</u> all the saved will spend eternity. Most people, when they hear the word "gospel," only think of someone preaching a salvation message. The gospel that Jesus preached had elements that were both present and future. The hope of salvation was always kingdom related and connected to the new earth referenced in Revelation 21. Christ's gospel was a kingdom gospel. Once saved, believers are called children of God and also <u>children of the</u> <u>kingdom</u>. Isn't that a blessing? It's an eternal connection to our Lord and Heavenly Father and our future *mansion* or dwelling place with Him. Take a look at the verses that bring this to light:

Matt 13:36-38

36 Then Jesus sent the multitude away, and went into the house: and his disciples came unto him, saying, Declare unto us the parable of the tares of the field.

37 He answered and said unto them, He that soweth the good seed is the Son of man;

38 The field is the world; the good seed are the <u>children</u> <u>of the kingdom</u>; but the tares are the children of the wicked one.

When Jesus preached the gospel of the kingdom, He did it with authority. He had the power to forgive sins, heal the sick, give sight to the blind, cleanse the lepers, cast out demons, rebuke the devil, calm the raging sea, and raise the dead. Now when that kind of a "man" preaches about His kingdom, the multitudes were pressing (running over) people to get to hear this gospel, good news. Luke 16:16: *The law and the prophets were until John: since that time the kingdom of God is preached, and every man presseth into it.* Wouldn't you? The thing that was not apparent to all of them was the nature of His kingdom and time that it would begin.

By the way, could I ask you a question? Feeling the sense that you are all shaking your heads yes, here's the question. When was the last time that you heard someone preaching the gospel that Jesus preached, i.e., the good news about His eternal kingdom of righteousness which shall begin in Revelation 21? It just might be that if an evangelist would begin preaching what God promised to those who would repent and follow the Savior, people now-a-days might start pressing to get into the kingdom also. Here's a look at the promise that Israel missed and perhaps the church has missed as well. The promise was given in Isa 65:17: *For, behold, I create new heavens and a new earth: and the former shall not be remembered, nor come into mind.*

We know that Jesus preached the kingdom of God and told the people how they could enter into it, for it is scattered through all the gospels. Towards the end of the book of Acts, we find the same gospel was heralded by the Apostle Paul. Acts 20:25: *And now, behold, I know that ye all, among whom I have gone preaching the kingdom of God, shall see my face no more.* Also, the last verse in Acts 28:31: *Preaching the kingdom of God, and teaching those things which concern the Lord Jesus Christ, with all confidence, no man forbidding him.*

The very last mention of the gospel being preached is found in this passage in Revelation 14:6: *And I saw another angel fly in the midst of heaven, having the everlasting gospel to preach unto them that dwell on the earth, and to every nation, and kindred, and tongue, and people.* This event will take place towards the end of the seven years of the great tribulation period. With this angel there is no mention of him having any lack of language skills. Every person on the earth will hear this gospel of the everlasting kingdom of Christ one final time before Armageddon. Then Jesus returns in Revelation 19 to begin His millennial reign.

For those who teach and preach that saved believers will spend eternity in heaven, it wonders one if they have somehow overlooked the Scriptures that speak of believers returning with Christ to reign with Him. Here are a few examples in Zechariah 14:5: *And ye shall flee to the valley of the mountains; for the valley of the mountains shall reach unto Azal: yea, ye shall flee, like as ye fled from before the earthquake in the days of Uzziah king of Judah: and the <u>LORD my God shall come, and all the saints with thee</u>.* This is also mentioned here in 1Thess 3:13: *To the end he may stablish your hearts unblameable in holiness before God, even our Father, at <u>the coming of our Lord Jesus Christ with all his saints</u>.*

It's not too late to start preaching the gospel that Jesus preached, the good news about God's eternal kingdom of righteousness in a newly created earth. A place where He will dwell with the children of the kingdom forever and make all things new.

57

KINGDOM INVITATION

Matt 22:1-3

1 And Jesus answered and spake unto them [the pharisees] again by parables, and said,

2 The kingdom of heaven is like unto a certain king, which made a marriage for his son,

3 And sent forth his servants to call them that were bidden to the wedding: and they would not come.

In the parable of the wedding feast, an invitation is extended by the king (God the Father) to whosoever will to come to His Son's (Jesus') wedding celebration. Jesus spoke this parable to the chief priests and the Pharisees. They were always trying to find some way to trap Him with their loaded questions. They hated Jesus like Cain hated Able. The enmity between the seed of the serpent and the seed of the woman represents an unbroken theme in human history that will remain until the end of Christ's millennial reign. This animosity finds its end when Satan and all of his seed are cast into the lake of fire.

Like Cain, who rejected God's offer of grace and forgiveness, the world has rejected God's kingdom message in pursuit of their own dark and evil ways. Jesus was talking to religious Jews who wanted the kingdom of Israel to be put back in a position of world authority. They wanted to be figures once again of power and dominance. All the good and godly things that Jesus did only angered them because it drew the people away from their heartless and empty words. Wow! Can't wait! How about you? *Thy kingdom come, the Spirit and the bride say, come!*

The Berean Principle

Be ready always! 1 Pet 3:15

Rightly dividing truth! 2 Tim 2:15

Acts 17:11
"... they received the word with all <u>readiness</u> of mind, and searched the scriptures daily, whether those things were so."
© BWCF

KINGDOM MESSENGERS

This chapter may prove to be extremely surprising to some and even amazing to others. To begin, think of the creation and then the conception of a soul and its eternal existence. You are one of those eternal souls. Think about how the Lord Jesus spoke to Adam and Eve in the paradise surroundings of the Garden of Eden. God Himself was the first Person to communicate with man. It was a perfect kingdom in a perfect world. It was the creation of heaven and earth where all things were new. Now think of the second time these words were spoken again to us. Rev 21:1,5:*1 And I saw a new heaven and a new earth: for the first heaven and the first earth were passed away; and there was no more sea. 5 And he that sat upon the throne said, Behold, I make all things new. And he said unto me, Write: for these words are true and faithful.*

Keep these thoughts and ponder just how wonderful that day will be. Now we are called to be the Lord's messengers. When Jesus and His disciples preached the gospel of the kingdom of God, this climatic chapter had not been written yet. John had the blessing of adding these final words to the Canon of Scripture. As kingdom messengers, we have the greatest hope, the greatest privilege, and the greatest responsibility to let the whole world know the reality of that hope. May we be as faithful, fearless, and fervent as those who we will learn about in this chapter of *Heaven and Beyond*.

The above chapter title, Kingdom Messengers, could also have been Kingdom Angels, for the word "angel" simply means messenger. The reason for the difference is interesting. That difference will be seen as the chapter unfolds.

The first reference to angels is found here in Gen 16:7 "And the angel (Strong's # 04397 *mal'ak*) of the LORD found her [Hagar] by a fountain of water in the wilderness, by the fountain in the way to Shur."

Types of Messengers

Messengers are both heavenly and earthly. Men are called angels and heavenly beings are called angels. Christ Himself is a Messenger for His Father. When

He speaks or appears before His incarnation, it is called a Christophany. Genesis 16:7 is the first of many examples that you will find in the Old Testament. Sometimes a messenger's or angel's presence is visionary (spirit like) and sometimes it is physical. At times, angels are men who have not experienced death. Then, at other times, angels are said to be men who have died and gone to be with the Lord in heaven, who serve as His messengers. Surprising, right?

For the creation and history of spirit heavenly creatures, there is little to be said in Scripture. Nevertheless, exploring this subject may be one of the most revealing, factfinding discoveries of a lifetime. Well, at least it was for me. At the end of each study, there will always be some unanswered questions. One in particular is if Gabriel is a created spirit being of highest ranking, then why does his name mean *man of God*? Once you understand the generic nature of angels, it will be a fascinating journey. Let's begin by asking some questions: What is the meaning of the word "angel" in the Bible? Are there different kinds of angels? What is a theophany or rather a Christophany? Are there different kinds of spirits? If so, what is the difference? When angels appeared to people, why did they have the appearance of men? What could it be like for Christians living after death as a spirit person? What will saved people be doing after death as spirits before their Christlike resurrection? When will the spirit and soul have a glorified body?

Holy angels have an important part in the welfare of believers. One day, in glory, we may have the blessing of meeting them in person and thanking them.

The way to start searching for answers is to use a Bible app that has a Strong's Concordance. It will give you the ability to see every place a word appears and what English word or words the translators used as its equivalent. Each Hebrew (OT) and Greek (NT) word has a Strong's number assigned to it. That number is always the same in every English Bible translation. Our goal is to see where the one Greek word may be translated a number of different English words. We are interested in learning who the angel is. Is the angel a person living or dead or is the angel a spirit creature that can appear as a human? Are you ready to start? Here goes!

Angel = (1. human type) a messenger — a person who speaks for God, i.e., prophet, priest, or king, a person of exemplary conduct (2. spirit type) spiritual being attendant upon God

Luke 9:52 *And sent **messengers** [Stg's # 32] before his face: and they went, and entered into a village of the Samaritans, to make ready for him.*

Rev 2:1 *Unto the **angel** [Stg's # 32] of the church of Ephesus write; These things saith he that holdeth the seven stars in his right hand, who walketh in the midst of the seven golden candlesticks.*

Angel Old Testament

"Strong's Hebrew word search for # 04397 in KJV from an unused root meaning to dispatch as a deputy; a messenger; specifically, of God, i.e. an angel (also a prophet, priest or teacher): – ambassador, angel, king, messenger."

Angel New Testament

"Strong's Greek word search for # 32 in KJV from *ang'-el-os* (probably derived from 71; compare 34) (to bring tidings); a messenger; especially an 'angel'; by implication, a pastor, angel, messenger."

Next, I used the English dictionary function in my Bible app and looked up the meaning of angel and found two types of angels listed.

After this, I looked for examples of both types in Scripture and here is what I found:

Living Human Messengers

Luke 9:52

And sent <u>messengers</u> [men] (Stg's #32 *ang'-el-os*) before his face: and they went, and entered into a village of the Samaritans, to make ready for him.

Rev 2:1 Unto the <u>angel</u> [the pastor] (Stg's #32 *ang'-el-os*) of the church of Ephesus write ...

Spirit Messengers — Angels of God

This group of angels has some of the most familiar passages that we identify with quickly. Angels are not only God's messengers, they are also our protectors.

Gen 28:12

And he dreamed, and behold a ladder set up on the earth, and the top of it reached to heaven: and behold the <u>angels of God</u> ascending and descending on it.

Gen 32:1

And Jacob went on his way, and the <u>angels of God</u> met him.

Matt 22:30

For in the resurrection they [men and women] neither marry, nor are given in marriage, but are as the <u>angels of God</u> in heaven.

Luke 12:8

Also I say unto you, Whosoever shall confess me before men, him shall the Son of man also confess before the <u>angels of God</u>:

Luke 15:10

Likewise, I say unto you, there is joy in the presence of the <u>angels of God</u> over one sinner that repenteth.

John 1:51

And he saith unto him, Verily, verily, I say unto you, Hereafter ye shall see heaven open, and the <u>angels of</u>

God ascending and descending upon the Son of man.

Heb 1:6

And again, when he bringeth in the firstbegotten into the world, he saith, And let all the angels of God worship him. {again ...: or, when he bringeth again}

Angel of the LORD

This phrase, angel of the LORD, is recorded some 60 times in Scripture. The first reference is a Christophany. A Christophany is a preexisting appearance of Christ, in human form, before His birth in Bethlehem. At times, it may be difficult to be certain that the phrase is a reference to Christ or simply an angel doing His will. The last reference appears in Acts and shows God's anger towards the wicked who think themselves worthy of praise that belongs only to God.

Gen 16:7

And the angel of the LORD found her [Hagar] by a fountain of water in the wilderness, by the fountain in the way to Shur.

Acts 12:23

And immediately the angel of the Lord smote him

[Herod], because he gave not God the glory: and he was eaten of worms, and gave up the ghost.

Angels of Renown

Dan 10:13

But the prince of the kingdom of Persia [Satan] withstood me [Gabriel] one and twenty days: but, lo, Michael [the Archangel], one [meaning there were more] of the chief princes, came to help me; and I remained there with the kings of Persia.

Dan 10:21

But I [Gabriel] will shew thee that which is noted in the scripture of truth: and there is none that holdeth with me in these things, but Michael [the heavenly archangel] your prince.

Jude 1:9

Yet Michael the archangel, when contending with the devil he disputed about the body of Moses, durst not bring against him a railing accusation, but said, The Lord rebuke thee.

Rev 12:7

And there was war in heaven: Michael [the heavenly

archangel] and his angels fought against the dragon [the devil]; and the dragon fought and his angels.

Messengers Who Appear as Men and Are Called Men

Dan 9:21

Yea, whiles I was speaking in prayer, even the <u>man Gabriel</u>, whom I had seen in the vision at the beginning, being caused to fly swiftly, touched me about the time of the evening oblation.

Gen 18:1-2

1 And the LORD appeared unto him [Abraham] in the plains of Mamre: and he sat in the tent door in the heat of the day;

2 And he lift up his eyes and looked, and, lo, <u>three men</u> [Christ and two angels] stood by him: and when he saw them, he ran to meet them from the tent door, and bowed himself toward the ground,

Gen 19:1,5

1 And there came two angels [the two men who were with the LORD] to Sodom at even; and Lot sat in the gate of Sodom: and Lot seeing them rose up to meet

them; and he bowed himself with his face toward the ground;

5 And they called unto Lot, and said unto him, Where are the men [the two angels] which came in to thee this night? bring them out unto us, that we may know them.

Earthly Messengers Who Appeared With Christ After They Died

Matt 17:3

And, behold, there appeared unto them Moses and Elias [they were alive] talking with him.

Old Testament Resurrected Saints

Matt 27:52-53

52 And the graves were opened; and many bodies of the saints which slept arose,

53 And came out of the graves after his [Christ's] resurrection, and went into the holy city, and appeared unto many.

These Old Testament Saints were messengers of the resurrection. It is a good thing to know that there is only one resurrection of the lost, but numerous resurrections of the saved. These living witnesses were the first to be resurrected after Jesus Christ. Many more will follow next at the rapture of the church. This will take place just before the beginning of the seven years of the great tribulation.

1 Thess 4:17

17 Then we which are alive and remain shall be caught up together with them in the clouds, to meet the Lord in the air: and so shall we ever be with the Lord.

Evil Spirits or Demons

In this group there are only bad messengers who are servants of the evil one. They are named as the devil, demons, and people — men and women who worship Satan, and who are possessed or controlled by evil spirits or the devil himself.

Since there is nothing good in the Scriptures about the bad messengers, we will just move on and leave them where they belong — unworthy of mention.

Ministering Spirits

Of all the verses that talk about angels, this one gives God's children the greatest feeling of comfort and security. It shows us that our Lord is ever present and ready to protect and save His children from danger.

Matt 18:10

Take heed that ye despise not one of these little ones [God's children]; for I say unto you, That in heaven their angels do always behold the face of my Father which is in heaven.

Have no fear for each child of God has a guardian angel waiting for his instructions to come to your rescue.

Heb 1:13-14

13 But to which of the angels said he at any time, Sit on my right hand, until I make thine enemies thy footstool? 14 Are they not all ministering spirits, sent forth to minister for them who shall be heirs of salvation?

Commentary Angel Confusion

I have saved this category for last. Commentators have made some remarks about angels that will not hold up under closer inspection. Those who have read these commentaries know what I am about to say. This is where the Berean principle and the context and harmony rules make the difference in the outcome.

The passages that come into play are found in Genesis Six, Job One, Two, and 38, and Jude. Let's take a look!

Gen 6:1-8

1 And it came to pass, when <u>men</u> began to multiply on the face of the earth, and daughters were born unto them,

2 That the <u>sons of God</u> saw <u>the daughters of men</u> that they were fair; and they took them wives of all which they chose.

3 And the LORD said, My spirit shall not always strive with man, for that he also is flesh: yet his days shall be an hundred and twenty years.

4 There were giants in the earth in those days; and also after that, when the <u>sons of God</u> came in unto the <u>daughters of men</u>, and they bear children to them, the same became mighty men which were of old, men of renown.

5 And GOD saw that the wickedness of man was great in the earth, and that every imagination of the thoughts of his heart was only evil continually.

6 And it repented the LORD that he had made man on

the earth, and it grieved him at his heart.

7 And the LORD said, I will destroy man [the seed of the devil, the wicked] whom I have created from the face of the earth; both man, and beast, and the creeping thing, and the fowls of the air; for it repenteth me that I have made them.

8 But Noah [the seed of the woman, the righteous] found grace in the eyes of the LORD.

What we learned in Gen 3:15 about the two seeds is now of upmost importance. We learned that there are only two groups of people in the world at all times throughout the Scriptures. There is the seed of the woman (the righteous) and the seed of the serpent (the wicked). *Men*, in verse one represents the wicked and *sons of God* in verse two represents the godly line of Seth who are the righteous. These *sons of God* committed spiritual adultery by marrying the daughters of men, [the wicked]. Verse five characterizes the result as hearts that were *only evil continually*. These *sons of God* in the family of the righteous became wicked. Because of this, God destroyed the world with

74

the great flood. Only one man of the *sons of God* and his family had remained faithful and his name was Noah.

The context has no mention of fallen spirits or demons that were somehow able to recreate themselves as men and father children with humans. This is what some of the commentaries have suggested. There is nothing in these verses to support that type of speculation.

Before moving on to the next passages, there are a few things to consider. What does *the way of Cain* represent in Jude 1:11? *Woe unto them! for they have gone in the way of Cain, and ran greedily after the error of Balaam for reward, and perished in the gainsaying of Core.* The way of Cain refers to all those who turn away from God. This would include any in the godly line of Seth or Abraham who reject God and His Word. Jesus said that people choose the wrong path because they love darkness more than light because their deeds are evil. This is a reflection once again back to Gen 6:5: ... *the thoughts of their hearts were only evil continually.* The Lord, in Matthew 23,

75

gave one of the most scathing rebukes to the sons of Abraham that was ever written. Although the sons of Abraham are viewed as God's children, this was conditional upon a spiritual new birth, right? This lesson Nicodemus learned from Jesus in John 3:1-7. All of this has been said to keep you from losing sight of this simple fact — there are only two groups of people in Scripture, the lost and the saved, the children of God and the children of the devil, the wheat and the tares, the sheep and the goats. The Lord expressed this truth in many different ways, but the reality is still the same.

As we move on to the next passages in Job, keep in mind who the sons of God are. They are the spirits of saved men who were in the paradise side of *sheol* or *Gehenna*. Jesus spoke of this place in Luke 16:19-31.

Job 1:6-7

6 Now there was a day when the sons of God came to present themselves before the LORD, and Satan came also among them.

7 And the LORD said unto Satan, Whence comest

thou? Then Satan answered the LORD, and said, From going to and fro in the earth, and from walking up and down in it.

Job 2:1

Again there was a day when the <u>sons of God</u> came to present themselves before the LORD, and Satan came also among them to present himself before the LORD. Admittedly, to explain outer space travel among spirits is a "leap in the dark" for anyone of us. We know that Gabriel was hindered in his travels to see Daniel, and Michael had to help him. So, we will just let the "how" up to God and move on from there, ok? What we do know is that on occasions the <u>sons of God</u> and Satan had an opportunity to present themselves before the LORD in heaven.

So, now we know that Old Testament Saints had the tremendous experience of visiting the third heaven and being in the very presence of God. Twice Scripture mentions that there was a day when this occurred. On those days, the Saints heard Satan, the accuser of the brethren, in action. Perhaps, they also had the blessing of seeing Job emerge victorious and God's double blessing in his last days. This reminds each of us to be like Job and remain faithful no matter what comes our way.

Job 38:7

When the morning stars sang together, and all the <u>sons of God</u> shouted for joy?

These are all the references to the *sons of God* in the entire Old Testament. There is absolutely nothing to indicate that the sons of God are anyone other than those of the godly line who were either faithful or unfaithful. In Hebrews, the question is asked, if angels were ever called the sons of God. Take a look: Heb 1:5: *For unto which of the angels said he at any time, Thou art my Son, this day have I begotten thee? And again, I will be to him a Father, and he shall be to me a Son?*

To help ourselves here a bit, let's state the golden rule of Bible interpretation which is: "When the plain sense makes common sense, seek no other sense." This simply means to take it literally. Before something can be used figuratively or symbolically, it must first be used literally. If a word is not used literally, the context will be the guide. When stars are said to be singing or rocks crying out, a figure of speech called a personification is replacing the literal sense in a poetical sense. How do we know this? Because stars and rocks cannot speak. Thus, we have the first part of Job 38:7: ...*the morning stars sang together*. In searching the Scriptures, no direct or indirect link was found to stars as angels, other than that angels sing. If you do a search for morning stars or stars sang, you will only find one, Job 38:7.

Another point of interest is that the chronology of events in Job 38 is random. The time and circumstances related to the event in verse seven is not given. Job was asked if he was there and knew what was happening. Job didn't and neither do we know the answer to God's question.

Sometimes the next passage is also linked to the commentary confusion about angels. They make the assertion that the angels spoken of here are the sons of

God in Genesis Six.

Jude 1:6

And the angels which kept not their <u>first estate</u>, but left their <u>own habitation</u>, he hath reserved in everlasting chains under darkness unto the judgment of the great day.

To start, let's get some clarity for *first estate* and *own habitation*.

> **first estate** = is only one word, *arche*. It can mean origin, time or rank. Well, there is nothing difficult about that.
>
> Strong's # 746. arch arche, ar-khay'
>
> **own habitation** = residence or house where God intended them to be.

Here are some examples of angels that had similar fears of receiving the same punishment after meeting Jesus.

Matt 8:29

And, behold, they cried out, saying, What have we to do with thee, Jesus, thou Son of God? art thou come hither to <u>torment us before the time</u>?

Luke 4:33-34

33 And in the synagogue there was a man, which had a spirit of an unclean devil, and cried out with a loud voice,

34 Saying, Let us alone; what have we to do with thee, thou Jesus of Nazareth? art thou come to destroy us? I know thee who thou art; the Holy One of God.

The sense of all this is that God never created these angels to possess people or animals. Some that left their first estate (original position) and destroyed people's lives by possessing them (their new residence or house) were kept in everlasting chains under darkness until the end of Revelation 20. Then they will be cast into the lake of fire with the devil and all of the other fallen angels and punished forever. To me, that is the end of the story about commentary angel confusion.

This was a most interesting study. I hope that it has encouraged you to use the Berean search method to get Bible answers. This is how to be a messenger of the Lord.

KINGDOM BRIDE

To begin this study, I did a search for bride in my Bible app. It responded with 14 hits. Here is the complete list: Isa 49:18; Isa 61:10; Isa 62:5; Jer 2:32; Jer 7:34; Jer 16:9; Jer 25:10; Jer 33:11; Joe 2:16; *Joh 3:29; Rev 18:23; *Rev 21:2; *Rev 21:9; Rev 22:17. The question that we would like the Scripture to answer is, "Who is the bride and wife of Christ?" The bride, the wife of Christ, is all those who are a part of His Body — the saints. The verses that are asterisked represent commentary confusion on the subject. This confusion is created when the word "bride" is used as a simile and the commentators use it literally. The verses that are underlined have a link to the answer in our question. All of the other references have no direct or indirect bearing on the subject in question.

He is an awesome God who numbered the stars and calls them all by name. If you will follow His words, the picture will not only be clear, it will be most spectacular. It will be like looking into the water on a bright sunny day and seeing the reflection of your own face in it.

Here are some of the key words that identify the bride, who are all saved people: *blood, white, linen, raiment, robes, garments, saints, bride, marriage, wife.* It all began with the first garments that God gave to Adam and Eve. Those garments represented Christ and His shed blood. Saints are described as having white garments of pure linen which pictures that believers have been made clean through the precious blood of Christ. Oh, wow! Do you hear all those people shouting and praising God? Some of their tears of joy are falling on the pages of this book right now. To God be the glory and worthy is the Lamb!

These are the Scriptures that answer the question, "Who is the bride and wife of Christ?" Be patient and spot each of the key words that identify His bride. This is how the Bereans searched the Scripture daily.

If you listen carefully, you will hear the voices of the saints throughout the ages. They are identified with the bride of Christ by their white robes and garments made from fine linen. What made them all clean and white was the blood of the Lamb of God, Jesus Christ.

1Sam 2:9

He [the LORD] will keep the feet of his saints, and the wicked shall be silent in darkness; for by strength shall no man prevail.

Matt 27:52

And the graves were opened; and many bodies of the saints which slept arose.

Dan12:10

Many shall be purified, and made white, and tried; but the wicked shall do wickedly …

Rev 3:5

He that overcometh, the same shall be clothed in white raiment …

Rev 6:11

And white robes were given unto every one of them; and it was said unto them, that they should rest yet for a little season, until their fellowservants also and their brethren, that should be killed as they were, should be fulfilled.

Rev 18:23-24

23 And the light of a candle shall shine no more at all in thee; and the <u>voice of the bridegroom and of the bride shall be heard no more</u> at all in thee: for thy merchants were the great men of the earth; for by thy sorceries were all nations deceived.

24 And in her [Babylon] was found the <u>blood</u> of <u>prophets</u>, and of <u>saints</u>, <u>and of all</u> that were slain upon the earth.

Rev 19:7-8

7 Let us be glad and rejoice, and give honour to him: for the <u>marriage of the Lamb</u> is come, and his <u>wife</u> hath made herself ready.

8 And to her was granted that she should be arrayed in <u>fine</u> <u>linen,</u> clean and <u>white:</u> for the <u>fine</u> <u>linen</u> is the <u>righteousness of saints.</u>

Rev 22:17

And the Spirit and **the <u>bride</u> [the saints from all ages in their white garments made clean by the blood of the Lamb]** say, Come. And let him that heareth say, Come. And let him that is athirst come. And whosoever will, let him take the water of life freely.

This great salvation began with Adam and Eve and ends with the last soul saved before Revelation 21. When people are born of the Spirit, they are called a child of God and children of the kingdom of God. Here is one example: Matt 13:38, *The field is the world; the good seed are the <u>children of the kingdom</u>* ...

Each of God's children have their name recorded in the Lamb's book of life (Rev 21:27). Are you sure that your name is written there?

The Berean Principle

Acts 17:11
"... they received the word with all <u>readiness</u> of mind, and searched the scriptures daily, whether those things were so."

KINGDOM SUPPER

By comparing Scripture with Scripture and keeping the context and harmony rules in play, the *supper* in Revelation 19 has a very different meaning than that which is presented in many of the commentaries. This *supper* is a celebration feast for the righteous. All the saints who suffered persecution by the wicked are about to see the fierceness and wrath of Almighty God unleashed upon their enemies. What follows is Armageddon. Those saints who are privileged to take part in this *supper* will see the wrath of God break the bands of the wicked. From the righteous blood of Abel to the last tribulation saint, there will be rejoicing. This *supper of the great God* takes place at the end of the seven years of tribulation and begins the 1000-year reign of Christ with His saints.

Jesus, as well as many other prophets, spoke of these events. Here are just a few passages that have a fitting place in the context which you are about to read in Revelation 19:7-9,17: *7 Let us be glad and rejoice, and* *give honour to him: for the <u>marriage of the Lamb</u> is come, and his <u>wife</u> hath made herself ready. 8 And to her was granted that she should be arrayed in fine linen, clean and <u>white</u>: for the <u>fine linen</u> is the <u>righteousness of saints</u>. 9 And he saith unto me, Write, Blessed are they which are called unto the <u>marriage</u> <u>**supper** of the Lamb</u>. And he saith unto me, These are the true sayings of God.*

*17 And I saw an angel standing in the sun; and he cried with a loud voice, saying to all the fowls that fly in the midst of heaven, Come and gather yourselves together unto <u>the **supper** of the great God</u>.*

The word "supper" is bolded in two places. It is important to understand its symbolic sense. In each verse, supper represents the time of God's vengeance against the wicked. The wife's readiness is described by her garment. The fine linen, clean and white, was made so by the blood of the Lamb and is said to be the righteousness of the saints. Hallelujah, praise the Lamb! All the saints who are called to be a part of this great event are those that God favored with this special blessing. They are all numbered in the *armies which were in heaven that followed Jesus upon white horses* as mentioned in Rev 19:14.

In Chapter Six, the souls of those who were slain for the Word of God cried out and said, "How long ...?" They wanted to know when their blood would be avenged. They were told that they had to *rest for a little season, until their brethren* should also be killed. That little while ended in Revelation 19:17 with *the supper of the great God.*

Here are some other verses which are linked to *the supper of the great God.*

Luke 17:36 Two men shall be in the field; the one shall be taken, and the other left.

37 And they answered and said unto him, Where, Lord? And he said unto them, <u>Wheresoever the body is, thither will the eagles be gathered together</u>.

Searching the Scriptures in reference to the bride of Christ has been very rewarding, at least to me and hopefully to you also. We now know that the bride of Christ or His wife is identified as saints with white garments of pure linen — the blood washed believers.

Rev 19:13 And he was clothed with a vesture dipped in blood: and his name is called The Word of God.

14 And the armies [the called in vs 9] which were in heaven followed him upon white horses, clothed in fine linen, white and clean [the saints, the bride of Christ].

15 And out of his mouth goeth a sharp sword, that with it he should smite the nations: and he shall rule them with a rod of iron: and he treadeth the winepress of the fierceness and wrath of Almighty God.

16 And he hath on his vesture and on his thigh a name written, KING OF KINGS, AND LORD OF LORDS.

17 And I saw an angel standing in the sun; and he cried with a loud voice, saying to all the fowls that fly in the midst of heaven, Come and gather yourselves together unto the supper of the great God.

Finally, there is an understanding from Scripture about the bride of Christ and the supper in Revelation 19. The bride of Christ is the redeemed. Those blood bought souls who surrendered their lives to Christ and kept His Word, some even unto death. An untold number of martyred saints are yet future, but in different parts of the world, they are being persecuted at this very moment. Their martyrdom is linked to a verse in Revelation 19 that speaks of the blessed that are called to the marriage supper of the Lamb. There are numerous verses that mention those who return with Christ at His second coming, but until now it was never clear to me who they were. The saints who suffered for Him will be called to the marriage supper and reign with Him for 1000 years. Here is the verse that mentions the *called* in Rev 19:9: *And he saith unto me, Write, Blessed are they which are called unto the marriage supper of the Lamb* ...

Here are some verses that are linked to suffering with Christ and reigning with Him:

2Tim 2:12

If we suffer, we shall also reign with him [Christ]: if we deny him, he also will deny us.

Rev 20:4

And I saw thrones, and they sat upon them, and judgment was given unto them: and I saw the souls of them that were beheaded for the witness of Jesus, and for the word of God, and which had not worshipped the beast, neither his image, neither had received his mark upon their foreheads, or in their hands; and they lived and reigned with Christ a thousand years.

As a part of the bride of Christ, we have been given great opportunities to occupy various positions of service in this life and in the afterlife. When a saint dies, it's not the end. It's the beginning. The beginning of an endless time filled with unimaginable rewards for those who have been faithful in doing God's will. Be not weary pilgrim in your journey, just keep your eyes on the Savior and His kingdom promises. Let us say with all of the bride, "Even so Lord Jesus, come!"

Rev 22:12 And, behold, I [Jesus] come quickly; and my reward [rewards are merit based] is with me, to give every man according as his work shall be.

Lord bless you dear brothers and sisters in Christ. It will be worth it all when we see Jesus and hear Him say, "Thou good and faithful servant well done, enter into the joy of the Lord."

KINGDOM HORSEMEN

This is an excellent time to refine our understanding of those which return with King Jesus at His second coming. He will return this time as the Man of war. These two verses set the stage for this great victory event between the righteous and the wicked, the seed of the woman and the seed of Satan. It is an encouraging thought to ponder during our present day when it seems like the whole world is against those who want to do right. There is a chance that some of you may be one of these horsemen. So, hang on to your hats and get ready to ride.

Rev 19:14 And the armies [saints and angels] which were in heaven followed him upon white horses, clothed in fine linen, white and clean.

Rev 19:19 And I saw the beast [the antichrist], and the kings of the earth, and their armies, gathered together to make war against him that sat on the horse, and against his army.

Knowing that Jesus is Yahweh/Jehovah is a key factor

in helping people who have been misled to believe that He is a created being. It is also important for Christians to see this truth vindicated many times in passages like this:

Zechariah 14:5 And ye shall flee to the valley of the mountains; for the valley of the mountains shall reach unto Azal: yea, ye shall flee, like as ye fled from before the earthquake in the days of Uzziah king of Judah: and the LORD [Yahweh] my God shall come, and all the saints with thee.

Now take a look at this same prophecy in the New Testament and connect the dots to Rev 19:14.

1Thess 3:13 To the end he may stablish your hearts unblameable in holiness before God, even our Father, at the coming of our Lord Jesus Christ with all his saints.

Jude 1:14 And Enoch also, the seventh from Adam, prophesied of these, saying, Behold, the Lord cometh with ten thousands of his saints.

Both saints and angels will return with Jesus at Armageddon. The fowls of the air will feast on their dead carcasses. This is the Revelation 19 supper. Here are some of the verses that mention angels returning with Him at the second coming:

Matt 25:31 When the Son of man shall come in his glory, and all the holy angels with him, then shall he sit upon the throne of his glory:

2Thess 1:7 And to you who are troubled rest with us, when the Lord Jesus shall be revealed from heaven with his mighty angels.

How would any of us have an opportunity to be in the Lord's army? This is more than just a song that little children sing, it's a genuine possibility for believers. Jesus said that people are called to this supper. He will call the faithful ones. The ones who loved Him enough not only to live for Him, but also to die for Him. That should not be a hard thing for any saint, right?

Christ will have an army of saints and angels. They will descend from heaven to earth in time to prevent Israel from being destroyed by the wicked. Be faithful pilgrims. Do what you know to be the Lord's will and then listen for the call to join His mighty army.

KINGDOM ENTRANCE

The kingdom entrance is still a mystery to many church people. What would you say to someone who asked you how to enter the kingdom of God? What passage of Scripture would you offer for an answer? Would you give a who or what answer to the question? What if the answer you gave to someone was the wrong answer? Would you say that my church has the right answer? If there are many wrong answers to this question, what is the right answer?

I can recall a recent conversation with a Muslim. During our discussion, Jesus was mentioned and he said that they had Jesus in their religion. The idea was that you have Jesus and we have Jesus, so we both must be all right. He said that God had been so good to him. Then he asked, "Why should I do anything different now?" This man had a wonderful loving family. He was a very successful business man and loved being kind to people. He was a man of faith in God. How could people like this not know the entrance to the kingdom of God? Let's take a look at some examples!

The Rich Young Ruler was a man that did not know the

answer to this question until he asked Jesus. Keeping

the law was no problem with him, for he told Jesus that

he had observed it from a youth. Because Jesus knew

his heart, like He knows yours and mine, He said in

Mark 10:21, *One thing thou lackest.* That one thing

may differ with various people, but it all boils down to

what Jesus said in these two verses:

Matt 16:25-26

25 For whosoever will save his life shall lose it: and

whosoever will lose [surrender] his life for my sake

shall find it.

26 For what is a man profited, if he shall gain the whole

world, and lose his own soul? or what shall a man give

in exchange for his soul?

What the Muslim man lacked was truth. Muslims do

not believe that Jesus is the Eternal Son of God and the

Creator of all things. The truth sets a person free and

Jesus said that He is Truth. When truth matters more

than anything else, people will find it. Nicodemus

learned that Jesus had the answer to the kingdom entrance question. This is what Jesus told him:

John 3:3-7

3 Jesus answered and said unto him, Verily, verily, I say unto thee, Except a man be born again, he cannot see the kingdom of God.

4 Nicodemus saith unto him, How can a man be born when he is old? can he enter the second time into his mother's womb [physical birth], and be born?

5 Jesus answered, Verily, verily, I say unto thee, Except a man be born of water [physical birth] and of the Spirit, he cannot enter into the kingdom of God.

6 That which is born [a child] of the flesh is flesh; and that which is born [born of God] of the Spirit is spirit.

7 Marvel not that I said unto thee, Ye must be born again [have a spiritual birth].

When a person has a second birth, that person becomes a child of God and a child of God's kingdom. The Holy Spirit indwells that person and enables him/her to walk in newness of life. The Word of God becomes the source of their strength and object of their obedience.

KINGDOM BODIES

What will kingdom bodies be like? Well ladies, this is your chapter. There will be no more need for dieting. There will be no more need for makeup or hair dye. Wow!! Can you hear the shouting and cheering? All of a sudden, every lady is turning to page 99. Someone must have put this on Facebook just moments ago. :) Perhaps the best answer to this question is that our glorified bodies will be perfect. Yes, our bodies will be sinlessly perfect in every way. We will then be as God intended us to be. Our fellowship with Him will never be hindered. He will be our God and we will be His people for time without end. Now that's something to look forward to and make us cherish even more the opportunities to layup treasures in heaven now.

The first piece of information about our kingdom bodies comes from a dialog that Jesus had with the Sadducees. They did not believe in the resurrection. So, they gave Jesus a "trick" question about the resurrection. The question was about a woman who had seven husbands. All her husbands died. Then they asked Jesus who would be her husband in the resurrection. This is what He said.

Matt 22:29-32

29 Jesus answered and said unto them, Ye do err, not knowing the scriptures, nor the power of God.

30 For in the resurrection they neither marry, nor are given in marriage, but are as the angels of God in heaven.

31 But as touching the resurrection of the dead, have ye not read that which was spoken unto you by God, saying,

32 I am the God of Abraham, and the God of Isaac, and the God of Jacob? God is not the God of the dead, but of the living.

Jesus made two points in His reply that help us with our questions about our kingdom bodies. The first point being that there will be no need for reproduction in God's eternal kingdom. The names written in the Lamb's book of life will fix the number for the kingdom population. When Jesus said that Abraham,

Isaac, and Jacob were alive, He made the second point. People that suffer a physical death are still alive in an intermediate state. Some of the details about it are given in Luke 16:19-31. Here Jesus gave an example of what happened to two people. One was lost and he was the rich man. The other was saved and he was the beggar. They both had life after death in *sheol* (the place where the souls and spirits of the dead went until the resurrection of Jesus). One side of *sheol* was a place of torment and the other side was paradise. Shortly after Jesus' resurrection, saints who died were said to be absent from the body and present with the Lord in heaven. 2Cor 5:8: *We are confident, I say, and willing rather to be absent from the body, and to be present with the Lord.*

We can learn some other things about our resurrected bodies from Jesus. After He was resurrected, He appeared to his disciples. To confirm to them that He was not a spirit apparition, this is what He said in Luke 24:36: *And as they thus spake, Jesus himself stood in the midst of them, and saith unto them, Peace be unto you. 37 But they were terrified and affrighted, and supposed that they had seen a spirit. 38 And he said unto them, Why are ye troubled? and why do thoughts arise in your hearts? 39 Behold my hands and my feet, that it is I myself: handle me, and see; for a spirit hath not flesh and bones, as ye see me have.* After Jesus showed them His hands and feet, He joined them in a meal of boiled fish and honeycomb.

We still know very little about a glorified body, yet we know that we will be like Jesus when we see Him. 1John 3:2: *Beloved, now are we the sons of God, and it doth not yet appear what we shall be: but we know that, when he shall appear, we shall be like him; for we shall see him as he is.* This has the implication that we will have flesh and bones. We will be able to eat food and possibly move from place to place like Jesus did by impulse.

The next group of Scriptures give us some amazing insight about our source of life. Are you ready? Hold onto your seats, for this is really fascinating to ponder. The Lord gave the Apostle Paul many facts about the resurrection. Let's review them one at a time and see what we can learn from 1Cor 15:

1Cor 15:35

But some man will say, How are the dead raised up? and with what body do they come?

The first thing to remember is that Paul is speaking to people that say there is no resurrection of the dead. He told them that if Jesus did not raise from the dead, then our faith is in vain. He begins by posing the how and what questions. He uses the example of a grain of wheat. It has to die first. Then that dead seed is planted. What comes to life and springs up through the ground is not the seed, for it has been changed into a living plant. This makes the point that our resurrected, glorified bodies will also be different from the bodies that we have now. How they will be different is the next point.

1Cor 15:42-44

42 So also is the resurrection of the dead. It is sown in corruption; it is raised in incorruption:

43 It is sown in dishonour; it is raised in glory: it is

sown in weakness; it is raised in power:

44 It is sown a natural body; it is raised a spiritual body. There is a natural body, and there is a spiritual body.

Now here is the major difference in the source of life for our natural body of flesh and our supernatural body of the spirit. The life of our fleshly bodies is in the blood. Lev 17:11: *For the life of the flesh is in the blood: and I have given it to you upon the altar to make an atonement for your souls: for it is the blood that maketh an atonement for the soul*. If the blood is removed from our bodies, we die. The source of life in our glorified bodies will be the presence of the Holy Spirit. He is the source of life in the saint's glorified body. The Holy Spirit abides with the child of God forever. That is why the Scripture says that we can never die. Take a look at these verses and let this truth bless your soul.

John 11:26

And whosoever liveth and believeth in me [Jesus Christ] shall never die. Believest thou this?

Never die means that we will never be separated from

God the Father, God the Son, and God the Holy Spirit again. Why? The next verse answers this question.

Joh 14:16

And I will pray the Father, and he shall give you another Comforter [the Holy Spirit], that <u>he may abide with you for ever</u>.

In the next verse, the Lord uses Paul's words to make this point clear:

1Cor 15:50-54

50 Now this I say, brethren, that <u>flesh and blood cannot inherit the kingdom of God</u>; neither doth corruption inherit incorruption.

51 Behold, I shew you a mystery; We shall not all sleep, but <u>we shall all be changed</u>,

52 In a moment, in the twinkling of an eye, at the last trump: for the trumpet shall sound, and the dead shall be raised incorruptible, and we shall be changed.

53 For this corruptible must put on incorruption, and this mortal must put on immortality.

54 So when this corruptible shall have put on incorruption, and this mortal shall have put on

immortality, then shall be brought to pass the saying that is written, Death is swallowed up in victory.

Victory in Jesus is what we as children of God's kingdom sing about all through this journey here. We know this is true, for Jesus said in Joh 14:19: *Yet a little while, and the world seeth me no more; but ye see me:* <u>*because I live, ye shall live also*</u>.

I don't know about you, but there's a longing to be absent for this body and to be present with Jesus that grows stronger each day. It makes me more determined to finish the work the Lord has given me. Not just to finish, rather to finish it with honor having kept the faith and run the race lawfully.

Knowing all this, Lord, please give us grace to run the race and to be the light that will lead those in darkness to You. Let us bid them to see Your nail pierced hands and riven side to hear Your kind words that say, "Come unto me, … and I will give you rest."

Thank You, Lord, for the promise of a glorified body and to be with You forever. Even so, Lord Jesus, come!

KINGDOM WITNESS

While what was learned about the Holy Spirit in the last chapter is still lingering, let's examine another aspect of His great influence. Those desiring a conscious awareness of God's presence know what is echoed in this text — Rom 8:16: *The Spirit itself <u>beareth witness with our spirit</u>, that we are the children of God: 17 And if children, then heirs; heirs of God, and joint-heirs with Christ; if so be that we suffer with him, that we may be also glorified together.* The inheritance that was promised to Christ was His eternal kingdom. This is fulfilled in the Revelation 21 prophecy. The eternal presence of the Holy Spirit in the saints is expressed as *Christ in us*. Take a look in Col 1:27: To *whom God would make known what is the riches of the glory of this mystery among the Gentiles; which is <u>Christ in you</u>, the hope of glory.*

When Jesus spoke of His sheep hearing His voice, this could be God speaking directly to a person like the Apostle Paul. It also could mean the Holy Spirit speaking to a person through his spirit. Philip is a good example in Acts 8:29: *Then the Spirit said unto Philip, Go near, and join thyself to this chariot. 30 And Philip ran thither to him, and heard him read the prophet Esaias, and said, Understandest thou what thou readest?* God can speak to people through the witness of the Holy Spirit whenever He chooses.

I remember a pastor telling the story of being in route to visit a church member. As he was driving, the Spirit told him to stop at the next house. He looked at the house and kept driving. The Spirit kept telling him to go back to that house. Finally, he turned around and went back. Looking in the window, he saw a person lying unconscious on the floor. To make a long story short, he learned that day (like Philip) to obey the voice and witness of the Holy Spirit. This is just one of many times that people have told me of similar experiences of the Holy Spirit speaking to them through their spirit. Since the Holy Spirit indwells every saint forever, He will be with us also during God's eternal kingdom. At this point, one could only speculate about the effects of this Holy Unction. Sometimes, I think of what John must have felt while his head was laying on the Lord's chest. This intimate contact with Christ came from a heart of love. Yet, when Christ ascended, that same intimacy was still possible through the Holy Spirit.

In God's eternal kingdom, saints will never quench or grieve the Holy Spirit. Surely, what a day that will be! The kingdom witness of the Holy Spirit will not only sustain us and be our source of life, it fills us with God's presence at all times. No wonder that Jesus preached the gospel (good news) of the kingdom of God. It really is the reality of our hope and salvation.

In leaving this wonderful thought of the Comforter's kingdom presence, we humbly pray as Jesus taught His disciples this prayer:

Luke 11:2

And he said unto them, When ye pray, say, Our Father which art in heaven, Hallowed be thy name. Thy kingdom come.

KINGDOM CITY

Much of the confusion about the kingdom city was already discussed in the introduction. This kingdom, holy city is said to be God's eternal dwelling place. Let's take a look at where this prophecy is mentioned. Then, see how God Himself makes this new Jerusalem His place to receive eternal glory.

Psa 132:13-14

13 For the LORD hath chosen Zion; he hath desired it for his habitation.

14 This is my rest for ever: here will I dwell; for I have desired it.

Zion is another name for Jerusalem. It will be destroyed along with this present earth and heaven. I have learned that this thought is immediately rejected by some believers. They protest by saying that this earth will be renovated, but not completely destroyed. Sorry folks, that's just not the case. Take a look in these Scriptures. John 18:36: *Jesus answered, My kingdom is not of this world: if my kingdom were of this world, then would my servants fight, that I should not be delivered to the Jews: but now is my kingdom not from hence.*

Why is Jesus' kingdom not of this world? Because this world will be destroyed, both the heaven and the earth. There are too many references to mention them all, but here are a few that should convince even the gainsayers.

Psa 102:25-26

25 Of old hast thou laid the foundation of the earth: and the heavens are the work of thy hands.

26 They shall perish, but thou shalt endure: yea, all of them shall wax old like a garment; as a vesture shalt thou change them, and they shall be changed.

This is a direct quote from Jesus: Matt 24:35: *Heaven and earth shall pass away, but my words shall not pass away.* In these verses, you will find some of the clearest and most direct statements about the earth's existence coming to an end. 2Pet 3:7: *But the heavens and the earth, which are now, by the same word are kept in store, reserved unto fire against the day of judgment and perdition of ungodly men.*

These next verses have literally caused panic among Jehovah's Witnesses when I asked them to read them to me: 2Pet 3:10: *But the day of the Lord will come as a thief in the night; in the which <u>the heavens shall pass away with a great noise,</u> and <u>the elements shall melt with fervent heat, the earth also and the works that are therein shall be burned up.</u> 11 Seeing then that <u>all these things shall be dissolved,</u> what manner of persons ought ye to be in all holy conversation and godliness, 12 Looking for and hasting unto the coming of the day of God, wherein the <u>heavens being on fire shall be dissolved,</u> and the elements shall melt with fervent heat? 13 Nevertheless we, according to <u>his promise, look for new heavens and a new earth, wherein dwelleth righteousness.</u>*

Now you will read what God gave the Apostle John to introduce Christ's eternal kingdom of righteousness: Rev 21:1: *And I saw <u>a new heaven</u> and <u>a new earth:</u> for the <u>first heaven and the first earth were passed away;</u> and there was no more sea.* Saints dwell there forever!

The verses that follow start the dialog about the new Jerusalem, God's eternal dwelling place. Rev 21:2: *And I John saw the holy city, new Jerusalem, coming down from God out of heaven, prepared as a bride adorned for her husband. 3 And I heard a great voice out of heaven saying, Behold, the tabernacle of God is with men, and he will dwell with them, and they shall be his people, and God himself shall be with them, and be their God.*

In light of all the other verses that we have already read, these two things should be absolutely clear. It should be clear that the holy city has been prepared as God's eternal tabernacle or dwelling place. It should be clear that the new earth and new heaven (atmospheric heaven) have been prepared as man's eternal dwelling place.

Well, some of you at this moment may be scratching your heads and wondering, right? To eliminate any confusion, let's take a look at *as a bride*, and *tabernacle of God* a little closer. *As a bride* is a simile, which is a figure of speech that compares the beauty of a bride to the beauty of the new Jerusalem. It is not saying that there is a bride in the new Jerusalem. For a long time, people have been misled by songs, commentaries, and preaching. They have been told that the church will dwell in the streets of gold and have mansions there in the holy city. Neither Revelation 21:2, or any other verse, in its proper context, teaches that. Here is what Scripture clearly teaches about the eternal dwelling place of the righteous, who are also called the bride, children of the kingdom, or simply, saints:

Ps 37:9,11,29

9 For evildoers shall be cut off: but those that wait upon the LORD, they shall inherit the earth.

11 But the meek shall inherit the earth; and shall delight themselves in the abundance of peace.

29 The righteous shall inherit the land [earth], and dwell therein for ever.

Matt 5:5

5 Blessed are the meek: for they shall inherit the earth.

Next, we will examine the texts that mention those who

were looking for the kingdom city. Many of these verses are found in this part of Hebrews:

Heb 11:10,16; 12:22; 13:14

10 For he looked for a city which hath foundations, whose builder and maker is God.

16 But now they desire a better country, that is, an heavenly: wherefore God is not ashamed to be called their God: for he hath prepared for them a city.

Note: God is the Maker who prepared them a city where He will dwell eternally so they can behold His glory and worship Him, according to Rev 21.

12:22 But ye are come unto mount Sion, and unto the city of the living God, the heavenly Jerusalem, and to an innumerable company of angels,

13:14 For here have we no continuing city, but we seek one to come.

Note: The continuing city is the new Jerusalem in Rev 21, where God will dwell forever. The gates will never be shut. The kingdom children of the nations will have continuous access to go in and out to worship Him at will. *And the Spirit and the bride say, Come!*

KINGDOM MANSIONS

You might begin by asking yourself where the idea of *mansions* originated. Yes, you're right! It comes from a passage in John 14. Why is it a common thought to jump immediately from *mansions* in John 14 to *the holy city* and *streets of gold* in Revelation 21? Well, it may be because many of the commentaries lead people in that direction. Let's take a look at how the Lord was leading the thoughts of His disciples and see where that will take us.

Perhaps, if we follow these verses more closely, we could avoid taking a leap in the wrong direction. If one keeps the Lord's comments in John 14:2-3 <u>in context with the surrounding chapters, the outcome will definitely be different</u> than leaping to Revelation 21. What context is that? It is the context of chapters 13, 14, 15, 16, and 17. If you do this, the Word will be rightly divided. If not, you will make the same mistakes many others have made. By comparing Scripture with Scripture and applying the context and harmony rules, you will be like the Bereans. It will prove to be interesting to see how the Berean's approach to Bible interpretation allows the true authority of Scripture to dominate the results.

Let's take a look at two sections of Scripture, John 14 and Revelation 21. These passages are often misrepresented by the commentaries and the people who use them. If we can examine these verses with a readiness to take God at His Word, the context and harmony rules will guide us to the right understanding.

Section One consists of the following verses:

SECTION ONE

Question

How and when did Jesus fulfill His three promises to the disciples in these two verses in John 14:2-3? What promises? His promises to prepare a place, to come again, and to receive them (His disciples) unto Himself in *a little while.*

John 14:2-3

2 In my Father's house are many mansions [Strong's # 3438]: if it were not so, I would have told you. I go to prepare a place for you.

3 And if I go and prepare a place for you, I will come again, and receive you unto myself; that where I am, there ye may be also.

John 14:23

Jesus answered and said unto him, If a man love me, he will keep my words: and my Father will love him, and we will come unto him, and make our abode [Strong's # 3438] with him.

Note: *Abode* in verse 23 [Strong's # 3438] is the same word as *mansions* in verse 2. What makes the difference is how the word is used. The part of speech, case, and number are different. It could be said that *homes* is equivalent to *mansions* in verse 2 and *home* is an equivalent to *abode* in verse 23.

Understanding the Father's House

If you were to do like the Bereans did, you would search the Scriptures for my Father's house, to see if it occurs anywhere else. Having done that, here is what you will find:

John 2:16

And said unto them that sold doves, Take these things hence; make not my Father's house an house of merchandise.

Note: When Jesus was talking about His Father's house in this verse, He was referring to the temple in Jerusalem. The temple area was a large complex. There were a number of structures connected to it and a part of it. This temple was the place of God's *shekhina* glory which represented His divine presence. *My Father's house* was a reference to God's earthly temple.

In John 14:2, the *Father's house* is a reference to the Father's current, heavenly dwelling place. It is the place where Jesus went at His ascension and is now sitting at the right hand of His Father. *The Father's house* is the heavenly temple that is described in these verses as the *third heaven* and called *paradise*.

2 Cor 12:2

2 I knew a man in Christ above fourteen years ago, (whether in the body, I cannot tell; or whether out of the body, I cannot tell: God knoweth;) such an one caught up to the <u>third heaven</u>.

3 And I knew such a man, (whether in the body, or out of the body, I cannot tell: God knoweth;)

4 How that he was caught up into <u>paradise</u>, and heard unspeakable words, which it is not lawful for a man to utter.

In Chapters 13, 14, 15, and 16, Jesus is preparing His disciples to understand that the people who hated and persecuted Him will do the same to them. Soon the disciples will be martyred. John is the only disciple who was not put to death. The Lord gave the Apostle John the book of Revelation and completed the canon of Scripture. What Jesus was saying to them in John 14:2-3 assured them that, after their death, they would be with Him in the third heaven where He would receive them. Take another look at verse 3 and connect the dots:

John 14:3

And if I go and prepare a place for you, I will come again, and receive you unto myself; that where I am, there ye may be also.

Understanding *If I Go*

This would be a good time to take a few moments and reread John 13-16. In these chapters, Jesus was preparing His disciples to be fearless, hated, comforted, persecuted, and martyred. This was no small task. He continued to convince them that His going would result in them being together again. He would come to them and then they would come to Him where He would be. He would receive them in *a little while.* In these verses, Jesus said that He was going to the Father and His going would result in them being with Him in a little while.

John 16:28

I came forth from the Father, and am come into the world: again, I leave the world, and go to the Father.

Note: Jesus, at His ascension, would go to the third heaven and sit at the right hand of His Father on the throne.

Understanding *I Will Come Again*

John 14:16-18

16 And I will pray the Father, and he shall give you another Comforter, that he may abide with you for ever;

17 Even the Spirit of truth; whom the world cannot receive, because it seeth him not, neither knoweth him: but ye know him; for he dwelleth with you, and shall be in you.

18 I will not leave you comfortless: I will come to you.

Note: Jesus would come to them. How would He do that? He would send the Comforter, the Holy Spirit, and He would abide with them forever. The Comforter's presence in a believer is said to be *Christ in you* according to Col 1:27: *To whom God would make known what is the riches of the glory of this mystery among the Gentiles; which is Christ in you, the hope of glory*. The Holy Spirit's presence in the saints is *Christ in you,* the hope of glory. This is how Jesus would come to His disciples in *a little while.*

This verse in John 17 gives more insight about Jesus' promise to come to His disciples. This chapter mentions oneness frequently. Jesus is praying to His Father concerning all those who are or will be saints.

John 17:26

And I have declared unto them thy name, and will declare it: that the love wherewith thou hast loved me may be in them, and I in them.

In verse 26, Jesus is praying about being one with the disciples and being in believers. If you look at Jesus' promise to come to those who are saved, you will find that it is linked to Him being in believers. He is in each person that is saved by means of the Holy Spirit.

Understanding In *A Little While*

As you read the words of Jesus in these verses, you will understand that in *a little while* was not a leap to Revelation 21 and the new Jerusalem. When the Apostles died, they would be present with the Lord in the third heaven. Jesus used His transfiguration scene to give them a preview of the afterlife by having Moses and Elias appear with Him. He taught them also that

123

the God of Abraham, Isaac, and Jacob was not the God of the dead, but the God of the living. Read now how Jesus explained *a little while* and assured the disciples that they would soon be with Him in His Father's house in the third heaven:

Understanding In *A Little While* — When?

John 14:19

Yet a little while, and the world seeth me no more; but ye see me: because I live [after death], ye shall live also [after death].

John 13:33,36

33 Little children, yet a little while I am with you. Ye shall seek me: and as I said unto the Jews, Whither I go [to the Father], ye cannot come; so now I say to you.

36 Simon Peter said unto him, Lord, whither goest thou? Jesus answered him, Whither I go, thou canst not follow me now; **but** thou shalt follow me afterwards [after you die].

John 16:16-19

16 A little while, and ye shall not see me [after His ascension]: and again, a little while, and ye shall see

me, because I go to the Father [they will be with Him there].

Understanding In *A Little While* — **Where?**

> 17 Then said some of his disciples among themselves, What is this that he saith unto us, A little while, and ye shall not see me: and again, a little while, and ye shall see me [Where? In heaven!]: and, Because I go to the Father?

Note: The "where" question in *a little while*, is answered in verse 17. Jesus is in the third heaven with His Father and the disciples will see Jesus there in heaven. Jesus has prepared a place for them THERE. *There*, meaning the third heaven? Yes, exactly! The when and where that Jesus would come are also a part of the context in these chapters. It is a fatal fault to move the when and where of John 14:3 to Revelation 21 and create a virtual illusion of it happening in the eternal state.

18 They said therefore, What is this that he saith, A little while? we cannot tell what he saith.

19 Now Jesus knew that they were desirous to ask him, and said unto them, Do ye enquire among yourselves of that I said, A little while, and ye shall not see me: and again, a little while, and ye shall see me?

Question Answered

The how and when question of Jesus' promises to His disciples in John 14:2-3 have been answered in the context of chapters 13-17 of John's gospel. The disciples, as well as other saints, are in the third heaven with Jesus now. He has prepared a place for each child of God. Being with Jesus after death, in the third heaven, is what gives every believer the hope and courage to face the hatred and persecution of this world. If you take the time to reread John 13-17, that warning of hatred and persecution will be resonating loud and clear in your mind and heart. Can't you feel that very atmosphere flooding our country even now? We can pray and ask the Lord to give us strength and grace to be peacemakers. People who have peace with God will have peace with themselves and with those around them. They will live in peace and die keeping the peace, if that's what it takes to bring honor and glory to their Savior.

SECTION TWO

Question

Why is it incorrect to make the promises that Jesus made to His disciples in John 14:2-3 to have their fulfillment in Revelation 21?

Rev 21:1-3

1 And I saw a new heaven and a new earth: for <u>the first heaven and the first earth were passed away</u>; and there was no more sea.

2 And I John saw the holy city, new Jerusalem, coming down from God out of heaven, prepared <u>as a bride</u> adorned for her husband.

Note: The new Jerusalem is described *as a bride* adorned for her husband. *As a bride* is a simile (a figure of speech). It is simply a poetical way of describing the beauty of the holy city. Those who make it *the bride* literally, make a grammatical error. The text is not saying that the new Jerusalem is the bride of Christ. This is where the commentaries and those who follow them misrepresent the Word of God and mislead His people. Matthew 5:19 says that those who mislead people will be the least in God's kingdom. Could you explain how that verse says that? Yes! We are told in 2Tim 2:15 to study to show ourselves approved unto God, workmen that needeth not to be <u>ashamed</u>, rightly dividing the word of truth. This is by no means one of the least of God's commandments. If a person misrepresents God's Word, he will be ashamed and wind up being the least in God's kingdom which begins in Revelation 21.

3 And I heard a great voice out of heaven saying, Behold, the tabernacle of God is with men, and he will dwell with them, and they shall be his people, and God himself shall be with them, and be their God.

Revelation 21 is the end and beginning. It is the end of this world and of all presences of all evil. What happened to this world? Verse 1 answered that question, as well as this passage:

2Pet 3:10-13

10 But the day of the Lord will come as a thief in the night; in the which the <u>heavens shall pass away</u> with a great noise, and the elements shall <u>melt with fervent heat</u>, the earth also and the works that are therein shall <u>be burned up</u>.

11 Seeing then that <u>all these things shall be dissolved</u>, what manner of persons ought ye to be in all holy conversation and godliness,

12 Looking for and hasting unto the coming of the day of God, wherein the <u>heavens being on fire shall be dissolved, and the elements shall melt with fervent heat</u>?

13 Nevertheless we, <u>according to his promise [Isa 65:17]</u>, look for <u>new heavens and a new earth, wherein dwelleth righteousness</u>.

The Promise

Isa 65:17

For, behold, <u>I create new heavens and a new earth</u>: and the former shall not be remembered, nor come into mind.

It has been my sad experience to have met so many people who have no or very little understanding of *Heaven and Beyond*. I have listened to preachers deliver messages at funerals for years that mislead people and give them false hopes. Telling people things about God and His kingdom that are not true can be corrected by doing what the Bereans did. They searched the Scriptures daily to see whether those things were so. You and I can do the same.

Answer

The answer to this question — "Why is it incorrect to make the promises that Jesus made to His disciples in John 14:2-3 to have their fulfillment in Revelation 21?" This interpretation would not follow the context or harmony rule. The time and place for their fulfilment would be misrepresented in both passages of Scripture. The place, the new Jerusalem, is prepared for God and His glory. The new, atmospheric heaven and earth are prepared for the saints, which are the *bride* of Christ. *The bride and the Spirit say come*; even so, come, Lord Jesus, and let Thy kingdom of righteousness begin.

KINGDOM ONENESS

Did you ever wonder what it will be like living in your glorified body? A body that will be in the likeness of our blessed Lord's. Well, if you did, you are not alone. King David had the same desire. Somehow, he had a certainty of waking up in glory and seeing his Lord. He said it so convincingly in Psa 17:15: *As for me, I will behold thy face in righteousness: I shall be satisfied, when I awake, with thy likeness.* David longed for a oneness with Yahweh, Jesus Christ, his Lord. He was not the only One who had that same longing for this oneness.

In John 17, Jesus prayed to His Father with a burden for this same oneness that David was seeking.

John 17:11,21-23

11 And now I am no more in the world, but these are in the world, and I come to thee. Holy Father, keep through thine own name those whom thou hast given me, that they [that's us] may be <u>one</u>, as we are.

21 That they all may be <u>one</u>; as thou, Father, art in me,

and I in thee, that they also may be <u>one</u> in us: that the world may believe that thou hast sent me.

22 And the glory which thou gavest me I have given them; that they may be <u>one</u>, even as we are one:

23 I in them, and thou in me, that they may be made perfect in <u>one</u>; and that the world may know that thou hast sent me, and hast loved them, as thou hast loved me.

Jesus expresses a oneness (a divine oneness) with His Father at different times. John 10:30 is one of those times: *I and my Father are one.* Immediately His hearers took offence. The Jews took up stones and would have killed Jesus right then and there, but it was not His time to die. Jesus asked them why they wanted to stone Him. The Jews knew the oneness that Jesus claimed with the Father made Him equal with God. This is what they said in John 10:33: *The Jews answered him, saying, For a good work we stone thee not; but for blasphemy; and <u>because that thou, being a man, makest thyself God</u>.*

This oneness, "How could we as lost sinners ever be

like Jesus and His Father?" Well, in God's kingdom of righteousness, it will be exactly that way — we will be one with God. We will no longer have a sinful nature. We will be like Jesus.

The Berean Principle

Be ready always! 1 Pet 3:15

Rightly dividing truth! 2 Tim 2:15

Acts 17:11
"... they received the word with all <u>readiness</u> of mind, and searched the scriptures daily, whether those things were so."
© BWCE

KINGDOM VICTORY

If you have been traveling down the road of new life in Christ Jesus for any length of time, you can remember some victory moments. It could be the day you were saved. My salvation victory day actually took place while driving to work one night in my truck. Well, at least I called it a truck (my El Camino). When the radio preacher said that some people are going to miss heaven by 18 inches, I didn't have a clue. Then he said that if you didn't understand that, you have only a head knowledge of God. The head is about 18 inches from your heart and you are lost and on your way to hell. When the radio preacher said that, the Holy Spirit spoke to me and said, "That's you!" At that moment, I knew that I was lost. During the invitation, the Lord showed me two things for the first time. I knew that it was my sins that Christ suffered for on the cross. And I knew that God loved me and gave His Son to die in my place. That moment, I surrendered my heart and life to Christ. With tears in my eyes, I began speaking to my Heavenly Father and said, "Lord I have lived 27 years of my life doing what I have wanted to do. But would You take my life now and use me to be a help and blessing to others?" From that night to this day, I continue my conversation with my Heavenly Father, my Blessed Lord Jesus, and my Ever-Present Comforter, the Holy Spirit. It was about a year later that the Lord spoke to me a second time, and called me to serve Him in the ministry. That was in 1974.

Since then, the victory moments continue to mount. My dear wife, "Putter," has written a book, *The Half Has Not Been Told* to describe many of those moments. She has a wonderful sense of humor and people just love it. She has a marvelous way of expressing it when she writes. When her pen dances across the paper, you're in for a joyful time of laughter and suspense. She will have you laughing one moment and crying the next. She has written *Putter's Pen*, her complement to our bimonthly prayer letter now for about 30 years.

Of all the victory moments in Scripture that anyone could speak of, there is one that outshines them all. It is tucked away in a passage that somewhat veils its glory. Putting this unsurpassable victory moment into the light is the intent of this chapter. Are you ready?

Understanding God All in All

Some years ago, a Sunday school teacher asked me if I could help him to understand a phrase in 1 Corinthians 15. That phrase is a part of this text in 1Cor 15:28: *And when all things shall be subdued unto him* [Jesus Christ]*, then shall the Son also himself be subject unto him* [God the Father] *that put all things under him* [Jesus Christ]*, that God* [God the Father, God the Son and God the Holy Spirit] *may be all in all.* The Sunday school teacher wanted to know the meaning of God being *all in all.*

God all in all is a kingdom victory that has its moment in Revelation 21. It may be important to catalog the verses in 1Cor 15 that lead up to this climatic phrase in verse 28. Many people get confused in reading this passage because of the pronoun and antecedent agreement. It is difficult to keep them connected. When I studied this text, many years ago, I asked my college English teacher to connect them for me. It's the only sure way of knowing who is saying what to whom. Did I say that right? LOL!

As you may very well know, the issue in this chapter is unbelief in the resurrection. Of course, without the resurrection, there is no Christianity. The gospel of the kingdom of God that Jesus preached is the promise of eternal life. If there is no life after death and Jesus was not resurrected, then there is no hope in this life or in the life to come. To stay focused on our main point, which is the meaning of *God all in all*, we will look for our answers in these verses:

1Cor 15:20-28

20 But now is Christ risen from the dead, and become the firstfruits of them that slept.

21 For since by man came death, by man came also the resurrection of the dead.

22 For as in Adam all die, even so in Christ shall all be made alive.

23 But every man in his own order: Christ the firstfruits; afterward they that are Christ's at his

137

coming.

24 <u>Then cometh the end,</u> <u>when he shall have delivered</u> <u>up the kingdom to God,</u> even the Father; when he shall have put down all rule and all authority and power.

25 For he must reign, till he hath put all enemies under his feet.

26 <u>The last enemy</u> that shall be destroyed <u>is death.</u>

27 For he hath put all things under his feet. But when he saith all things are put under him, it is manifest that he is excepted, which did put all things under him.

28 And when all things shall be subdued unto him, then shall the Son also himself be subject unto him that put all things under him, that <u>God may be all in all.</u>

To understand the phrase *God may be all in all* we must see the transition of power from one member of the Godhead to the other. When you see that, you will understand *God all in all.* The next thing is the timing. <u>When</u> does the merger of diverse positions and authority in the Godhead terminate? It ends when death is destroyed. At that time, all the fullness of the Godhead will be in the glorified body of Christ and diversity of positions, e.g., advocate, intercessor, and comforter will end and God will be *all in all*. This takes place in the new Jerusalem.

The end takes place at the end of Revelation 20. This earth is completely destroyed and all the evil spirits and the unsaved people are in the lake of fire. The new beginning takes place in Revelation 21 when it says that God creates a new earth and new atmospheric heaven. This begins the eternal kingdom of righteousness. At that time, there will be no more death. The destruction of death is the kingdom victory that will be everlasting. God will make all things new and the children of the kingdom live in the newly created earth forever. The fullness of God in the visible presence of Jesus, in the new Jerusalem, will be the kingdom's majesty. Jesus, our Lord and Savior, will be the object of everyone's worship and praise for time without end. This is when God is *all in all*.

KINGDOM WATER

You may be thinking that this is a strange chapter title in the kingdom dialog. Are you a bit puzzled about how the author will follow up on this subject? As you grow older in the Lord, did you ever think that God could stop amazing you? Well, I know that some of you may have been there, but are ever so amazed when you turn the next page of your Bible and find yourself just totally astounded at God's awesomeness. You've been there, right? This verse is one that has that effect each time I read it. It's the verse in Psa 147:4 that says, *He telleth the number of the stars; he calleth them all by their names.* How many stars is that? Man does not have numbers large enough to even reach the half-way mark of such as number as that. Our God is so wonderful, so awesome, so loving, so gracious, so caring, so forgiving, so incredible, so personal that He knows every hair on our heads. That's an awesome God! I am so thankful that He is my God, my Savior, my Shepherd, and my Friend … Aren't you? Now as you turn the page, let's take a look at the verse that speaks about water in God's eternal kingdom that begins in Revelation 21.

Rev 21:1

And I saw a new heaven and a new earth: for the first heaven and the first earth were passed away; and there was <u>no more sea</u>.

I could not tell you how many times that I have read this verse and never thought about the last three words, *no more sea*. Finally, when I did see this rather shocking statement, my curiosity became thirsty. I knew that *Siri* could quickly give me some answers. You know who *Siri* is don't you?

The National Ocean Service soon appeared on the screen of my iPhone. The first fact that they mentioned was that there is only one global ocean. This ocean covers about 71% of the earth's surface. Wow! That's a lot of water. This one world ocean is divided into five ocean basins. The modern-day ocean boundaries are called the Arctic, Atlantic, Indian, Pacific, and Southern. The Pacific Ocean basin is the largest of them all. It has been said that one could take all of earth's continents and they would fit into the Pacific Ocean basin. Amazing, right?

Now, *no more sea* is a remarkable contrast to this present world where we live. If there were mansions for every believer somewhere in the new earth, just think how much larger they became with *no more sea*. Another thought that is reasonable is who is to say that God could not have created the new earth and heaven much larger than the first one. Do you feel that bit of amazement that God can put into just three words, *no more sea*?

If you would like to give your imagination boundless limits, then think of what our Blessed Lord Jesus is saying in these verses:

Rev 21:5

And he that sat upon the throne said, Behold, <u>I make all things new.</u>

All things new is part of knowing the reality of our hope. It is what makes the saints long for God's kingdom and causes us to pray — Thy kingdom come!

KINGDOM GREATNESS

Did you ever read a passage that puzzled you about who's going to be the greatest or least in the kingdom? Just to be sure that we are thinking about the same thing, this is a reference to the eternal kingdom that begins in Revelation 21. James and John stirred the indignation of the other ten quickly by asking to sit on Jesus' left and right hand in His kingdom. This is perhaps one of the texts that would come to mind first to many. It does give us an indication that there will be rank and file in the new earth. This whole line of thought subjects us to self-examination. Hmm, do you wonder about your place in the new earth? If you are in the habit of comparing yourself to the Bible greats and feel left out, then get some comfort from this passage that always has intrigued me.

Before we go any further, please note once again, in the verses that follow, the use of *kingdom of heaven* in Matthew and the *kingdom of God* in Luke and the other gospel accounts. Matthew is writing to the Jews who were looking for their kingdom to be restored by Jesus' Messiahship to Israel. They wanted it to occur to free them from Roman domination. This is the last question that the disciples asked Jesus before He ascended in Acts 1:6: *When they therefore were come together, they asked of him, saying, Lord, wilt thou at this time restore again the kingdom to Israel?* At that time, they still did not understand that Jesus' kingdom would not be on this earth. Jesus made this clear in His words to Pilate here in John 18:36: *Jesus answered* [Pilate], *My kingdom is not of this world: if my kingdom were of this world, then would my servants fight, that I should not be delivered to the Jews: but now is my kingdom not from hence.*

Matt 11:11

Verily I say unto you, Among them that are born of women there hath not risen a greater than John the Baptist: notwithstanding he that is least in the kingdom of heaven is greater than he.

Luke 7:28

For I say unto you, Among those that are born of

women there is not a greater prophet than John the Baptist: but he that is least in the <u>kingdom of God</u> is greater than he.

John was the greatest man born of a woman in his standing as a prophet, yet anyone of us which are children of the kingdom, will be greater than him. This is an amazing statement. Have you ever pondered the truth of all this? It sounds to me like we all have an excellent chance to be something great in God's kingdom. How would you go about doing that? Well, just give someone a cup of water in Jesus' name for starters. Remember what He said in Mark 9:41: *For whosoever shall give you <u>a cup of water to drink in my name,</u> because ye belong to Christ, verily I say unto you, <u>he shall not lose his reward.</u>*

That should get you started. And this is a good time to thank each of you who have prayed and given to help make our 36 years of ministry possible. We remember the many times you invited us into your homes, served us a great meal, and helped to further our journey. Well, great will be your rewards in the *new earth*.

KINGDOM GARMENTS

Choosing a title for this chapter was somewhat difficult. Each title that was considered seemed a bit heartless. I was feeling the pain of this person's disappointment when he was rejected. Then I was thinking of how thankful I am to be one with the right garment. You will understand what I mean as soon as you read this text in Matt 22:11-13: *And when the king came in to see the guests, he saw there a man which had not on a wedding garment: 12 And he saith unto him, Friend, how camest thou in hither not having a wedding garment? And he was speechless. 13 Then said the king to the servants, Bind him hand and foot, and take him away, and cast him into outer darkness; there shall be weeping and gnashing of teeth.*

This passage is a part of Jesus' dialog where He was teaching the people. He spoke a parable with an application that showed why people would miss out on being in the kingdom. The Revelation 21 kingdom of righteousness.

The king, in the parable, planned a marriage for his son. He sent his servants to invite his guests to attend, but they would not come. Again, he sent other servants with an invitation saying that everything was ready for the wedding feast. Some thought little of it and went their way. But the remaining guests were hateful. They treated the king's servants wrongly and killed them. When the king heard this, he was furious and sent his armies and destroyed every one of those wicked men. The king told his servants to go out in the streets and invite as many as they could find to the marriage.

The people in the parable, which rejected the king's invitation, represented Israel as a nation. The guests which came, represented the who-so-ever-will may come. These guests were said to be both good and evil. As the story continues, the king came to see who had come and saw a man without a wedding garment. When the king asked the man how he got in without a wedding garment, he was speechless. This is an example of kingdom rejects. They represent people who think of themselves as destined for the kingdom, but will lack the white robe of righteousness that Christ has provided for His kingdom children.

Here is a passage which makes this point very clear. Lord, please help everyone reading these verses to be sure that they are not being described in what they read.

Kingdom Rejects

Matt 7:21-23

21 Not every one that saith unto me, Lord, Lord, shall enter into the kingdom of heaven; but he that doeth the will of my Father which is in heaven.

22 Many will say to me in that day, Lord, Lord, have we not prophesied [preached and testified] in thy name? and in thy name have cast out devils [done miracles]? and in thy name done many wonderful works?

23 And then will I profess unto them, I never knew you: depart from me, ye that work iniquity.

The kingdom, with its newly created heaven and earth, with all things made new and a beauty beyond imagination, with the Creator who is not ashamed to be called our God, is just too much for you to miss.

There is another condition that Scripture mentions with reference to those who enter or do not enter the kingdom. It is the love test. The last verses in Matthew Five talk about it and also 1John Four.

<u>Not Loving the Lost</u>

Matt 5:43-47

Ye have heard that it hath been said, Thou shalt love thy neighbour, and hate thine enemy.

44 But I say unto you, <u>Love your enemies</u>, <u>bless them that curse you</u>, <u>do good to them that hate you</u>, and <u>pray for them which despitefully use you, and persecute you</u>;

45 That ye may be the <u>children of your Father</u> which is in heaven: for he maketh his sun to rise on the evil and on the good, and sendeth rain on the just and on the unjust.

46 For if ye love them which love you, what reward have ye? do not even the publicans the same?

47 And if ye salute your brethren only, what do ye more than others? do not even the publicans so?

Not Loving Christian Brothers and Sisters

1John 4:20

20 If a man say, I love God, and hateth his brother, he is a liar: for he that loveth not his brother whom he hath seen, how can he love God whom he hath not seen?

The love doctrine is described in 1Corinthisns 13 with 16 points that tell what charity does. It also gives seven warnings about not having charity. When Jesus was asked to give the greatest commandment, this is what He said:

Matt 22:37-39

37 Jesus said unto him, Thou shalt love the Lord thy God with all thy heart, and with all thy soul, and with all thy mind.

38 This is the first and great commandment.

39 And the second is like unto it, Thou shalt love thy neighbour as thyself.

The "love garment" is what every person will need to enter the kingdom. It is provided by Jesus Himself. He invites you to come. Please, don't wait any longer!

KINGDOM LONGING

One malefactor, the thief on the cross who repented, asked Jesus to remember him when He would come into His kingdom. The Lord's reply may have been somewhat surprising, for Jesus said that he would be with Him that very same day in paradise. To many, knowing Jesus resulted in a longing to be with Him and like Him. This man's wait for the blessed hope was undoubtedly painful; nevertheless, unexpectedly short. What are your feelings about being absent from the body and present with the Lord? Do you have a compelling desire to go now or are you content with life here? Many Christians have fear of the unknown aspects of the afterlife. This can push the blessedness of our hope far from our thoughts. That is unless you could have seen what the Apostle Paul saw. He may have put it in a riddle, but many believe that he was speaking of himself in this passage in 2Corinthians 12:2-4: *I knew a man in Christ above fourteen years ago, (whether in the body, I cannot tell; or whether out of the body, I cannot tell: God knoweth;) such an one caught up to the third heaven. 3 And I knew such a man, (whether in the body, or out of the body, I cannot tell: God knoweth;) 4 How that he was caught up into paradise, and heard unspeakable words, which it is not lawful for a man to utter.*

The *unspeakable words* are what capture our imaginations. Did Jesus tell the Apostle Paul all about the kingdom? Did He give him a glimpse of the new earth and the skies above it? Could he have seen the new Jerusalem and the glory of Christ that lighted the entire city? Those questions remain unanswered, yet we know he had a longing to depart and be with the Lord. These verses in Philippians 1:23-24 tell the story: *For I am in a strait betwixt two, having a desire to depart, and to be with Christ; which is far better: 24 Nevertheless to abide in the flesh is more needful for you.* Yes, he had a longing to go, but he knew that the Lord had a work for him to finish and he put all of his heart and mind into doing it. He served the Lord with gladness and counted all things but loss to do it. Amen!

There are two other people who had a great longing to see the Lord. It is heartwarming to hear them speak of it. The Lord gave each of them the desires of their heart. Why wouldn't He do the same for you or me? The answer is that He will and He does. Hallelujah!! The first person is Simeon. The beginning of his story is found in Luke 2:25-26: *And, behold, there was a man in Jerusalem, whose name was Simeon; and the same man was just and devout, waiting for the Consolation of Israel: and the Holy Ghost was upon him. 26 And it was revealed unto him by the Holy Ghost, that he should not see death, before he had seen the Lord's Christ.*

Simeon was a man that studied the Scriptures and had a longing in his heart to see Jesus before he died. God was pleased to grant him that wish. Can you imagine that? I know that many of you are perhaps praising the Lord at this very moment, because He has given you the desires of your heart so many times. Well, I know that my heart is overwhelmed with joy, for that is my testimony. Some of the moments are just unspeakable.

Anna, the next person, is also found in Luke Two. This time, it is a wonderful, godly lady of prayer named *Anna, a prophetess.* She is truly a very remarkable person. We are told that *she was of a great age.* She could have been anywhere between the age of 84 to 105. Perhaps her deeds, in many ways, are unmatched anywhere else in Scripture. She was there in the temple at the same time as Simeon. She begins talking about Jesus to those looking for the *redemption* (the Messiah) in Jerusalem. This is found in Luke 2:38: *And she* [Anna] *coming in that instant gave thanks likewise* [the same as Simeon] *unto the Lord, and spake of him* [Jesus] *to all them that looked for redemption in Jerusalem.* How blessed that moment must have been for the Lord, Joseph, Mary, and these two aged saints of God.

David, a longing soul who will find no satisfaction until he sees Jesus. When you read Psalm 17:15, somehow you know it's David speaking before you look at the heading. *As for me, I will behold thy face in righteousness: I shall be satisfied, when I awake, with thy likeness.* Can you feel his passion? This is the man after God's own heart. He had a longing that could not be satisfied until he would be with his Lord.

When David is spoken of, some folks immediately think of his great sins. But aren't we glad that nothing can separate us (a child of God) from the love of God in Christ Jesus? We all at times need to be reminded of this great truth. Rejoice with me here in Romans for a few moments in verses 8:35, 37, 38, 39.

35 Who shall separate us from the love of Christ? shall tribulation, or distress, or persecution, or famine, or nakedness, or peril, or sword?

37 Nay, in all these things we are more than conquerors through him that loved us.

38 For I am persuaded, that neither death, nor life, nor angels, nor principalities, nor powers, nor things present, nor things to come,

39 Nor height, nor depth, nor any other creature, [nothing] shall be able to separate us from the love of God, which is in Christ Jesus our Lord.

David is satisfied now. He's with Him and like Him.

KINGDOM PARABLES

This chapter is one that creates a lot of interest. The Lord promised the disciples that these parables would reveal to them the mysteries of the kingdom. Everybody loves a good mystery, right? There are too many kingdom parables in the gospels to cover all of them. Books of great substance have been written on this subject and it's not my desire to cross that ocean. We will look at three aspects of the kingdom parables that relate to Revelation 21. They are salvation, stewardship, and treasure parables. Take a minute to grab a drink and your favorite snack and let's go.

Salvation Parables

With these parables, the Lord taught His disciples who is going to be in the kingdom of God and who isn't. He began with the parable of the sower and so will we. Before we begin, it might be good to understand what a parable is. It is a figure of speech. A figure of speech is simply a poetical way of expressing a literal truth. A parable uses physical circumstances to present a spiritual truth. That truth always has a literal application, e.g., the rich man and Lazarus — one tormented, the other blessed in the afterlife. This is the difference between a lost person and a saved person. All figures of speech have a literal application. This is important to know and to teach to others.

Parable of the Sower

This parable is recorded in all the synoptic gospels. It talks about four soils. The soil is a symbol for the heart. The heart is the seat of one's affection. From it flow the issues of life. It's what makes people different. When the seed (God's Word) is received by the fourth soil, pay close attention to the condition of that heart. If you do this, you will begin to understand the greatest lesson on salvation that Jesus ever taught. Are you ready? Ok, let the action begin!

Introduction Verses

When the disciples asked Jesus to explain this parable, note what He said in Mark 4:13: *And he said unto them, Know ye not this parable? and how then will ye know all parables?* Understanding the parable of the sower is the key to understanding all the kingdom parables. Why is that? It clarifies what Jesus already taught about the *straight and narrow way* and *few there be that find it*. What do you mean by that? The parable shows that the condition of one's heart is what makes the difference when making a profession of faith. The *good and honest heart* in the fourth soil is the only one that continued in the Word and had a desire to keep it. There is no continuance of the Word in the first three soils. That's why this parable was first and foremost. If His disciples did not understand this, they would not understand the doctrine of salvation and people would miss the kingdom of God.

Soil One — No Permanence of the Word

Luke 8:11-12

11 Now the parable is this: The seed is the word of God.

12 Those by the way side are they that hear; then cometh the devil, and taketh away the word out of their hearts, lest they should believe and be saved.

The desire to be forgiven and have peace with God is what keeps the Word in a lost person's heart. It stays!

Soil Two — No Permanence of the Word

Mark 4:16-17

16 And these are they <u>likewise</u> which are sown on stony ground; who, when they have <u>heard the word</u>, immediately receive it with gladness;

17 And have no root in themselves, and so endure but for a time: afterward, when affliction or persecution ariseth <u>for the word's sake</u>, immediately <u>they are offended</u>.

Likewise links the second soil to the first in that the Word had no permanent place in their hearts. To avoid affliction and persecution, their "Christianity" vanished. The Word in them and abiding is what gives a saved person roots. When there are no roots, profession without possession is what results.

Soil Three — No Permanence of the Word

Mark 4:18-19

18 And these are they which are sown among thorns; such as <u>hear the word</u>,

19 And the cares of this world, and the deceitfulness of riches, and the lusts of other things entering in, <u>choke</u>

159

the word, and it [the Word, not the person] becometh unfruitful.

It is the Word of God that transforms a person's mind and enables that person to become fruitful. When the Word is choked out, it is because the heart has no real desire to keep it. The Bible is on the shelf instead of abiding in the heart. This identifies a lost person, not a backslidden Christian.

Soil Four — Permanence of the Word

Luke 8:15

But that on the good ground are they, which in an honest and good heart, having heard the word, keep it, and bring forth fruit with patience.

Take a look at Jeremiah 29:13: *And ye shall seek me, and find me, when ye shall search for me with all your heart.* Although this verse is spoken directly to Israel, in application it applies to anyone who seeks God with an honest and good heart.

Knowledge is what a person knows. It is the first step in possessing the Word. The second step is the Word possessing you. You can't have one without the other.

Parable of the Wheat and the Tares

In Matthew 13, the Lord began teaching His kingdom parables. The sower parable was the first kingdom lesson on salvation. In the same chapter, He followed with the second lesson and explains it here.

Matt 13:36-39

36 Then Jesus sent the multitude away, and went into the house: and his disciples came unto him, saying, Declare unto us the parable of the tares of the field.

37 He answered and said unto them, He that soweth the good seed is the Son of man;

38 The field is the world; the good seed are the children of the kingdom; but the tares are the children of the wicked one;

39 The enemy that sowed them is the devil; the harvest is the end of the world; and the reapers are the angels.

We are reminded here once again that there are only two people groups in the world. The seed of the woman and the seed of the devil. The parable of the wheat and the tares is just another example of this truth. The difference here is that the tares are in the church.

In the parable of the sower, soils two and three are examples of the tares among the wheat. This same idea is expressed in Psalms One. It is in the last three verses: *4 The ungodly are not so: but are like the chaff which the wind driveth away. 5 Therefore the ungodly shall not stand in the judgment, nor <u>sinners in the congregation of the righteous</u>. 6 For the LORD knoweth the way of the righteous: but the way of the ungodly shall perish.* Oh, Lord, thy kingdom come!

Stewardship Parables

Did you ever wonder what your position will be in God's kingdom? The disciples did. At times, they even argued and fussed with each other about it. It's very strange, for now-a-days it is seldom mentioned. One reason may be because many people never think beyond heaven. The truth about the kingdom of God for the most part has disappeared. People think that they are going to spend eternity in heaven where Jesus is now. Or they think of heaven as the new Jerusalem and they will spend eternity there. Neither is true. Stewardship parables give information about your

162

position in the kingdom's new earth. The new Jerusalem is prepared for Christ and it is His eternal dwelling place in the kingdom of righteousness. The stewardship parables give us glimpses of kingdom positions. These positions are merit based. Knowing God's will for your life and doing it is how the positions are granted. One of the clearest examples is given when the Lord said that we should occupy till He comes. Occupy gives the sense of doing business. To us, that's gospel business. The Great Commission is God's gospel business for the church. So, with that in mind, let's get started and learn about kingdom stewardship.

The Talent Parable

When we read this parable, remember that the term kingdom of heaven is unique to Matthew's gospel. In like passages in Mark, Luke, and John, it is the kingdom of God. Making them two different places would be a mistake and misrepresent the context as a whole. With that in mind, let's get started.

Matt 25:14-30

14 For the kingdom of heaven is as a man travelling into a far country, who called his own servants, and delivered unto them his goods.

To shorten the 15 verses or more, we can summarize the story and examine the outcome. One servant was given five talents. To another two and the third servant, he was given one talent. The number of talents was based on each person's *several ability*. When the travelling man returned, after a long time, he reckoned with his servants. The first gained five. The second gained two, and the third gained none, because he buried his talent in the ground. The lord of the servants was pleased with the first two, but was angry with the person that did nothing.

28 Take therefore the talent from him [the one who did nothing], and give it unto him which hath ten talents.

29 For unto every one that hath shall be given, and he shall have abundance: but from him that hath not shall be taken away even that which he hath.

30 And cast ye the unprofitable servant into outer darkness: there shall be weeping and gnashing of teeth.

If this talent was gold, it would have been worth millions. The value of the talent relates to the great responsibility the church has in doing the Lord's business until He returns. What has He given us that is so valuable? He has given us the gospel of the kingdom. Do you remember reading about the gospel that Jesus preached? What gospel am I talking about? This one in Mark 1:14: *Now after that John was put in prison, Jesus came into Galilee, preaching the gospel of the kingdom of God, 15 And saying, The time is fulfilled, and the kingdom of God is at hand: repent ye, and believe the gospel.* The gospel of the kingdom is about Revelation 21 and the good news about a new earth where He will make all things new. A perfect place to live forever with perfect people, where the glory of God is visible continually with Jesus in the midst of the new Jerusalem. That's the talent that Jesus gave to the church. The idea behind the value of the talent is that it was worth so much that it was priceless. It may be that someone like you will revive the kingdom gospel and glorify King Jesus. Will you?

The Pound Parable

The most drastic difference between the talent and pound parables is the difference in value. A pound had the worth of a day's wages. Some estimate it to be about 16 dollars. Other variations have to do with the number of recipients, the number that was reckoned with, and each servant was given the same amount; one pound. The number of recipients was 10, but only three were asked to give an account.

Another interesting thing to recognize is the audience: the people that Jesus was speaking to. The talent parable is in the context of Matthew 24 and 25 when Jesus was specifically teaching His disciples. The pound parable was given during Jesus' journey to Jericho. When Jesus commanded Zacchaeus to come down out of the tree, the onlookers began to murmur. Jesus then spoke the parable because *they* (Luke 19:11) *thought that the kingdom of God should immediately appear.* To these people, a pound represented the wage of a hard day's work. Remember, Jesus knew their thoughts. Part of the lesson in the pound parable corrected their wrong thinking. Perhaps the parable could do the same for anyone who does not know the reality of their kingdom hope. If that applies to any of you, would you ask the Lord right now to give you that understanding?

I did not summarize the parable to shorten the text as before. Please take the time to read through it. And especially look at the difference in the two parables with the person which did nothing with his talent or pound. Ok, let's unfold the Scroll and see what the blessed Holy Spirit will give each one of us.

Luke 19:12-26

12 He said therefore, A certain nobleman went into a far country to receive for himself a kingdom, and to return.

13 And he called his ten servants, and delivered them ten pounds, and said unto them, Occupy till I come.

14 But his citizens hated him, and sent a message after him, saying, We will not have this man to reign over us.

15 And it came to pass, that when he was returned,

having received the kingdom, then he commanded these servants to be called unto him, to whom he had given the money, that he might know how much every man had gained by trading.

16 Then came the first, saying, Lord, thy pound hath gained ten pounds.

17 And he said unto him, Well, thou good servant: because thou hast been faithful in a very little, have thou authority over ten cities.

18 And the second came, saying, Lord, thy pound hath gained five pounds.

19 And he said likewise to him, Be thou also over five cities.

20 And another came, saying, Lord, behold, here is thy pound, which I have kept laid up in a napkin:

21 For I feared thee, because thou art an austere man: thou takest up that thou layedst not down, and reapest that thou didst not sow.

22 And he saith unto him, Out of thine own mouth will I judge thee, thou wicked servant. Thou knewest that I was an austere man, taking up that I laid not down, and

reaping that I did not sow:

23 Wherefore then gavest not thou my money into the bank, that at my coming I might have required mine own with usury?

24 And he said unto them that stood by, Take from him the pound, and give it to him that hath ten pounds.

25 (And they said unto him, Lord, he hath ten pounds.)

26 For I say unto you, That unto every one which hath shall be given; and from him that hath not, even that he hath shall be taken away from him.

The Lord's command was to occupy until He come. To occupy means to do business. Our "business," as Christians, is to tell people around us about King Jesus and His gift of salvation that makes every believer a child of His eternal kingdom. He will create a new earth and make everything there new. Read Revelation 21 as many times as it takes to see its beauty and feel the inward peace of becoming a sinless being. Those in His kingdom will be like Him in absolute sinless perfection. If we know the reality of our hope, it will become a beam of light so bright that others will also long to be in that kind of place.

One's faithfulness to the Lord's command to share the kingdom gospel with people everywhere will determine your place in Christ's kingdom. If you were to look up the rewards in Scripture, you will find many places that God has promised to reward your good works and your good words to others about the kingdom.

The stewardship parables encourage us to take what the Lord so richly has given us and share it in love with others. Telling people about a new world where there will be no sin will draw lost souls to the Savior. Yes, there is a heaven that awaits us when we die, but the eternal dwelling place of the saved is the new earth and all its beauty and glory. This is the gospel of the kingdom that Jesus preached about and the same message that His disciples preached. In the last verse of Acts, Paul was preaching the kingdom of God in Acts 28:31: [Paul] *preaching the kingdom of God, and teaching those things which concern the Lord Jesus Christ, with all confidence, no man forbidding him.*

Treasure Parables

There are two treasure parables in Matthew 13 that set the stage for where we're headed now. In this verse, Jesus gives us something important to remember. It's in Luke 12:34: *For where your treasure is, there will your <u>heart</u> be also.* We learn from this that hearts and treasures are both in the same place. Jesus also told us to *lay up treasures in heaven.* When a person does this, God will reward that person and, in some cases, they are greatly rewarded. Many of these rewards are future and connected to the eternal kingdom in the new earth. Still, there is somewhat of a mystery in all this. What are treasures and what are rewards? Jesus answered the treasure question one time when He said this in Luke 18:22: *Sell all that thou hast, and distribute unto the poor, and <u>thou shalt have treasure in heaven</u>: and come, follow me.* The Apostles made the mark here and possibly many of you which surrendered to do God's will. The mystery is starting to fade a bit, right?

Let's take a look at the two kingdom treasure parables and then, hopefully, the mystery will vanish. The first

171

one is here in Matthew 13:

Matt 13:44

Again, the kingdom of heaven is like unto treasure hid in a field; the which when a man hath found, he hideth, and for joy thereof goeth and selleth all that he hath, and buyeth that field.

Was it worth it all, you might ask this man? This could be his reply, "Just take a look around here and see what all I have now. I am living in a newly created earth and the sky above me is more beautiful than anything I've have ever seen. Jesus is here in the new Jerusalem. He is our God and we are His people. All things have become new and perfect. Yes, it was worth it all, for my treasure has become my reward."

Rev 21:1-3

1 And I saw a new heaven and a new earth: for the first heaven and the first earth were passed away; and there was no more sea.

2 And I John saw the holy city, new Jerusalem, coming down from God out of heaven, prepared as a bride adorned for her husband.

3 And I heard a great voice out of heaven saying, Behold, the tabernacle of God is with men, and he will dwell with them, and they shall be his people, and God himself shall be with them, and be their God.

The second treasure parable is found here:

Matt 13:45-46

45 Again, the <u>kingdom of heaven</u> is like unto a merchant man, seeking goodly pearls:

46 Who, when he had found one pearl of great price, went and <u>sold all that he had</u>, and bought it.

Both of these parables show the heart of the man. There was nothing that he possessed which had more worth to him than the kingdom. The pearl of great price is Jesus and His kingdom. Jesus talks here about the great loss suffered by those which value this world and the stuff they have more than their own souls. He said this in Matthew 16:25-26: *For <u>whosoever will save his life shall lose it</u>: and whosoever will lose his life for my sake shall find it. 26 For what is a man profited, if he shall gain the whole world, and lose his own soul? or <u>what shall a man give in exchange for his soul</u>?* The last interesting thing connected to all this is rewards. How does one get them and how do you keep them? If you do a search in your Bible app for rewards, you may find over 100 references. The first mention of rewards is found here in Genesis 15:1: *After these things the word of the LORD* [Yahweh] *came unto Abram in a vision, saying, Fear not, Abram: I am thy shield, and thy exceeding great reward.* Maybe you were thinking about mansions or, like the disciples, a position of power and permanence? This idea that our treasure is our reward is definitely a part of what Jesus is telling Abraham in this verse.

Are you wondering why I said Jesus here instead of Jehovah, or more correctly, Yahweh? Jesus is Yahweh. Of the nearly 7,000 times that the divine name is used in the Old Testament, 99% of the time it is referring to Jesus. Every one ought to know who Jesus is, right?

In a kingdom there is rank and file — different levels of authority. Positions of authority are a part of the rewards promised to those which are obedient and faithful in doing God's will. What do you mean? Well, look at the beatitudes. There are nine of them. Jesus said that there are rewards for doing them. He taught that here in Matthew 5:11-12: *Blessed are ye, when men shall revile you, and persecute you, and shall say all manner of evil against you falsely, for my sake. 12 Rejoice, and be exceeding glad: for <u>great is your reward in heaven</u>: for so persecuted they the prophets which were before you.* The mystery here is that the Lord does not mention what the rewards are. I am sure that each one of us would like to hear the Lord say to us these words, "Well done, good and faithful servant; thou hast been faithful over a few things, I will make thee ruler over many things: enter thou into the joy of thy Lord." The longing to hear these words is what keeps a child of God pressing on and seeking victory in every trial. It's what drives one to his knees and keeps him crying for forgiveness and grace to finish well.

So, we have learned that there are rewards, but now we will see that rewards can be lost because of disobedience to God's will. There is the possibility to be great in God's kingdom or to be the least. The least people are mentioned in this verse in Matthew 5:19: *Whosoever therefore shall break one of these least commandments, and shall teach men so, he shall be called the <u>least in the kingdom of heaven</u>* .... This verse is certainly an attention grabber for anyone in ministry who is preaching or teaching God's Word without a proper understanding of hermeneutical rules. Surely, God's command to rightly divide (correctly interpret) His Word is not one of the least of His commandments. Such a careless approach to ministry could cause one to lose rewards. We are encouraged in this verse to stay the course and do right that we may keep our reward. It's in 2John 1:8: *Look to yourselves, that we <u>lose not</u> those things which we have wrought, but that we <u>receive a full reward</u>.*

In closing our look at kingdom parables, we get a little closer to the big picture God paints about our future home in His kingdom. The reality of our hope continues to get brighter as the Lord brings each of us another day closer to our kingdom *place*.

KINGDOM MILLENNIUM

What is the millennial kingdom of Christ? It is His 1000-year reign, on this earth, that precedes the eternal kingdom of righteousness that begins in Revelation 21. During the millennial kingdom there will be sin, death and destruction. Political parties will not be in control. Religious parties will not be demanding their rights to worship their gods. It will be the time when this verse has its fulfillment in Philippians 2:10: *That at the name of Jesus every knee should bow, of things in heaven, and things in earth, and things under the earth; 11 And that every tongue should confess that Jesus Christ is Lord* [Yahweh], *to the glory of God the Father.*

The millennial reign of Christ begins at the end of the seven-year great tribulation period. The verse that gives the three divisions of Revelation is found in this verse, Revelation 1:19: [John] *write the* <u>*things which thou hast seen,*</u> *and the* <u>*things which are,*</u> *and the* <u>*things which shall be hereafter.*</u> The first division is *the things which thou hast seen.* It is in the past tense and covers

177

the unveiling of Christ in chapter one. The second division is *the things which are*. This is in the present tense and covers the letters to the seven churches in Asia Minor in chapters two and three. The third division is *the things which shall be hereafter*. It is in the future tense and it covers chapter four to the end of the book. Chapters four and five describe things before the throne. Chapters six through 18 cover the seven years of the great tribulation. Chapter 19 is the second coming of Christ and Armageddon. Chapter 20 is the millennium, the 1000-year reign of King Jesus, the final judgment, and the destruction of this present earth and heaven. Chapters 21and 22 begin Christ's eternal kingdom of righteousness and the eternal state. If one does not try to interpret the symbolism at various places, the book of Revelation is simple to understand. Here's a breakdown of the book at a glance.

1) Chapter 1 — The Unveiling of Christ

2) Chapters 2-3 — Letters to the Seven Churches

3) Chapters 4-5 — Before the Throne

4) Chapters 6-18 — The Great Tribulation

5) Chapter 19 — Christ's Second Coming and Armageddon

6) Chapter 20 — Christ's 1000-year Reign, the Final Judgment, the Lake of Fire, and the Destruction of this Earth and Heaven

7) Chapters 21-22 — The New Earth and the New Atmospheric Heaven, Christ in the New Jerusalem, and the Eternal Kingdom of Righteousness and the Eternal State

Our Father in heaven, Hallowed be thy name. Thy kingdom come. When this prayer is burning in the heart of every child of God, the things of this world will grow strangely dim. A longing for the Lord's physical, eternal presence in our lives will make our hearts ready and willing to serve Him with eagerness and joy. The beatitudes will become our attitudes. The Lord's desire for His children to be the salt of the earth and the light of the world will be a reality.

Christians have the greatest opportunity now to shine as lights in the midst of a crooked and perverse world. Our days are all numbered. Let's make them count.

KINGDOM WORSHIP

Do you ever feel hindered and sometimes almost frozen when it comes to worshiping the Lord? I do. Don't we long for true worship? Worship that is in and completely of the Holy Spirit. I can remember times during Bible college that worship was spontaneous. God didn't come down as some people say. We came up. People raised to their feet. Raised their hands. They lifted their voice with tears streaming down their cheeks and praised the Lord with clean hearts and joyful words of thanksgiving. No one was out of place by trying to speak their mind in rebuke to others. No one grabbed the microphone to preach his or her sermonette. All things were in order and the flow of worship was natural from hearts overflowing with the goodness of the Lord. At its best, all of these treasured moments were short lived. As many of those precious saints slipped into heaven, the spirit of worship they offered to God diminished. It was never something that came down. This worship came up from loving hearts.

Worship in the new earth, in new glorified bodies like our Lord's, with nothing to hinder will be one of the things that Jesus makes new in every child of the kingdom. Oh, my soul, even so, Lord Jesus, come! Maybe looking at these verses in Revelation will do something to see the beauty of worship in a new light.

Rev 21:23-27

23 And the city had no need of the sun, neither of the moon, to shine in it: for the glory of God did lighten it, and the Lamb is the light thereof.

24 And the nations of them which are saved shall walk in the light of it: and the kings of the earth do bring their glory and honour into it [this is the kind of worship that we long to offer to our Savior].

25 And the gates of it shall not be shut at all by day: for there shall be no night there.

26 And they [the saints] shall bring the glory and honour of the nations into it.

27 And there shall in no wise enter into it any thing that defileth, neither whatsoever worketh abomination, or maketh a lie: but they which are written in the Lamb's

book of life.

Rev 22:1-5

1 And he shewed me <u>a pure river of water of life, clear as crystal</u>, proceeding <u>out of the throne of God and of the Lamb</u>.

2 In the midst of the street of it, and on either side of the river, was <u>there the tree of life</u>, which bare twelve manner of fruits, and yielded her fruit every month: and the leaves of the tree were for the healing of the nations.

3 And <u>there shall be no more curse</u>: but the throne of God and of the Lamb shall be in it; and his servants shall serve him:

4 And <u>they shall see his face</u>; and his name shall be in their foreheads.

5 And there shall be no night there; and they need no candle, neither light of the sun; for <u>the Lord God giveth them light: and they shall reign for ever and ever</u>.

May the Lord help us to keep the thought of seeing His Face in our hearts. This day will surely come. It is what we sing about and the beautiful place where we long to be. It's that *prepared place*.

KINGDOM MEALS

This chapter will prove to be illuminating and edifying to some. To others, well, it may take a little longer for them to connect the dots, but if they do as the Bereans did, I believe the results will agree with what is about to be read. Just think, one day you (all the saints) will be at the Lord's table and eating this meal with Him. Hallelujah, Amen, and glory to God!

Meals is plural because there are three. Actually, only two meals that are kingdom meals and the other is the supper meal. The <u>millennial meal</u> takes place on this earth. The <u>kingdom meal</u> takes place in the new earth (Rev 21). The <u>supper meal</u> takes place at the end of Armageddon, just before the millennium begins.

They are discovered by searching for words like kingdom, table, supper, eat, and bread. Please keep this in mind! The kingdom of God is the eternal kingdom of righteousness.

Please remember that the kingdom of heaven in Matthew is parallel with the kingdom of God in Mark,

Luke, and John. For this reason, they cannot be divided into two different places or realms. Some of the confusion that exists comes from placing kingdom events in the millennial period. During the 1000-year reign of Christ, there will be sin, death, and destruction on this earth. In the kingdom period, this earth no longer exists. It will have been completely destroyed. All things will have been made new and sin is gone forever. This is our inheritance with Christ and what we are all longing for, right?

The Kingdom of God Meal

The kingdom of God is the simplest of the two kingdom meals to find and understand. So, let's start there and see what our searches for the key words reveal. The Lord's supper gives the key information that places this meal in the kingdom of God (Revelation 21). Take a look at these verses:

Matt 26:26-29

26 And as they were eating, Jesus took bread, and blessed it, and brake it, and gave it to the disciples, and said, Take, eat; this is my body.

184

27 And he took the cup, and gave thanks, and gave it to them, saying, Drink ye all of it;

28 For this is my blood of the new testament, which is shed for many for the remission of sins.

29 But I say unto you, I will not drink henceforth of this fruit of the vine, until that day when I drink it new with you in my Father's kingdom.

Verse 29 gives us another piece of information that is important to see. What's that? Jesus spoke of the kingdom of God (Revelation 21) as His Father's kingdom.

Luke 22:16-18

16 For I say unto you, I will not any more eat thereof, until it be fulfilled in the kingdom of God.

17 And he took the cup, and gave thanks, and said, Take this, and divide it among yourselves:

18 For I say unto you, I will not drink of the fruit of the vine, until the kingdom of God shall come.

The Millennial Meal

Perhaps, what you are about to read may be a missing link in the chain of end times events. Read these verses carefully and note how the timeline places them in the millennium period.

Luke 22:29-30

29 And I appoint unto you [the disciples] a kingdom, as my Father hath appointed unto me;

30 That ye may eat and drink at my table in my kingdom, and sit on thrones judging the twelve tribes of Israel.

How do we know that these verses are describing things in the millennial kingdom (1000-year reign of Christ) rather than the kingdom of righteousness? The answer to that question is underlined in verse 30. Judging the tribes of Israel is the reason. In the kingdom of righteousness, everything is perfect and no judging will ever be necessary. Praise the Lord, Amen!

The Supper Meal

The supper meal takes place at the end of the seven-year great tribulation period. Armageddon ends this period with Christ and His army breaking the bands of the wicked until the near end of the millennium. The saints of God have been waiting for this event since

Cain slew Abel. The great victory is but moments away. The enmity between the two seeds (the seed of the woman, the righteous, and the seed of Satan, the wicked) will finally favor the righteous. Through all the ages, the wicked have persecuted the righteous because they hated God. Listen to the cry of all the fallen from Abel to the last tribulation saint, which refused to take the mark of the beast. They mount their white horses and wait for the Captain of their Salvation to sound the trumpet. In these verses that you are about to read, the voice of a great multitude, and much people begin to build their joy for this long-awaited event. Take a look in Rev 19:1-6:

1 And after these things [the fall of Babylon, the power of Satan] I heard a great voice of much people in heaven, saying, Alleluia; Salvation, and glory, and honour, and power, unto the Lord our God:

2 For true and righteous are his judgments: for he hath judged the great whore, which did corrupt the earth [from Adam to that day] with her fornication, and hath avenged the blood of his servants at her hand.

187

3 And again they said, <u>Alleluia</u>. And <u>her smoke rose up</u> <u>for ever and ever</u>.

4 And the four and twenty elders and the four beasts fell down and worshipped God that sat on the throne, saying, Amen; <u>Alleluia</u>.

5 And a voice came out of the throne, saying, Praise our God, <u>all ye his servants</u>, and ye that fear him, both small and great.

6 And I heard as it were the voice of a <u>great multitude</u>, and as the voice of many waters, and as the voice of mighty thunderings, saying, <u>Alleluia</u>: for the Lord God omnipotent reigneth.

If you start reading in the beginning of Revelation 18, you will see these words in Revelation 18:2: *And he cried mightily with a strong voice, saying, <u>Babylon the</u> <u>great is fallen, is fallen</u>, and is become the habitation of devils, and the hold of every foul spirit, and a cage of every unclean and hateful bird.* The long-awaited day of <u>punishment</u> for the wicked has come. The four alleluias, in the beginning of chapter 19, express the joy of the saints throughout the ages. This is their day of seeing justice for the empire of evil. All of this is being said to encourage you to stay with the context as the supper meal comes into view. Supper is mentioned twice in Revelation 19. Both times it is speaking of the same event. If supper is disconnected, that context is lost. This is where the Berean principle is seen at its greatest value. It is also important to give precedents to the rules of interpretation and allow their referees to drop flags on positions that are out of bounds. Truth matters more than anything else, right?

Soon you will be reading verses that mention the bride and wife of Christ. These words must be understood in their relationship to the family of God. Hold on to your hats, your thinking hats, for these thoughts may be new to many of you. The essence of what will be said comes from the words in Ephesians chapters two through five. The mystery of the church is explained as a paradox of two becoming one. Take a look in Ephesians:

Eph 3:14-15

14 For this cause I bow my knees unto the Father of our

Lord Jesus Christ,

15 Of whom the whole family in heaven and earth is named.

Eph 4:4-6

4 There is one body [Christ's body], and one Spirit [the Holy Spirit], even as ye are called in one hope [the kingdom hope] of your calling;

5 One Lord, one faith, one baptism,

6 One God and Father of all [the saints], who is above all, and through all, and in you all.

Eph 5:30

30 For we [all saints] are members of his [Christ's] body, of his flesh, and of his bones.

31 For this cause shall a man leave his father and mother, and shall be joined unto his wife, and they two shall be one flesh.

32 This is a great mystery: but I speak concerning Christ and the church.

The Family of God

The unity that exists among all saints is the family unity. They are all called the children of God. The mystery of the church is described in the example of a husband and wife becoming one flesh. In the human family, there is only one body of which all are descendants from Adam. They are all part of his body. Adam is the head of that body.

In Jesus Christ, there is only one body (Eph 4:4) and that body is His body, which was crucified at Calvary. Every saint from Adam to the last soul that will be saved is a part of His body. That's what Scripture calls being in the family of God. The New Testament church, without question, is the body of Christ. It joined His body and has been given a special place in the family of God that is unique.

God only has one bride who became His wife and their relationship will never be severed. That metaphor represents the saints of all ages. Now, let's take a look at the supper meal in Revelation 21.

The church, as a part of the family of God, is the Lamb's wife, and the bride of Christ. It is with all saints a part of Christ's body. The army that returns with Christ in Revelation 19 are members of His body.

He said all those which suffered with Him would reign with Him. See the dots connected on page 216!

After the fourth alleluia, there was a voice that came out of the throne that said, "Praise our God, all ye his servants, and ye that fear him, both small and great." And then in verse seven the great multitude began to rejoice to honor Him, for the judgment for the wicked is about to take place.

Rev 19:7-9

7 Let us <u>be glad and rejoice</u>, and give honour to him: for the <u>marriage of the Lamb</u> is come, and his <u>wife</u> hath made herself ready.

8 And to her [the wife, people described in verses 1-6, and verse 8] was granted that she [the wife] should be arrayed in <u>fine linen</u>, clean and white: for the fine linen <u>is the righteousness of saints</u>.

9 And he saith unto me, Write, Blessed are <u>they which are called</u> unto the marriage <u>supper</u> of the Lamb.

There are some questions that must be asked at this point. Where is the next verse, in this chapter, that mentions the supper? It is verse 17. Is this supper the same supper that is mentioned in verse nine? The context offers no other answer but yes. Take a look!

Rev 19:11-17

11 And I saw heaven opened, and behold a white horse; and he that sat upon him was called Faithful and True, and in righteousness he doth judge and make war.

12 His eyes were as a flame of fire, and on his head were many crowns; and he had a name written, that no man knew, but he himself.

13 And he was clothed with a vesture dipped in blood: and his name is called The Word of God.

14 And the armies which were in heaven followed him upon white horses, clothed in fine linen, white and clean.

15 And out of his mouth goeth a sharp sword, that with it he should smite the nations: and he shall rule them with a rod of iron: and he treadeth the winepress of the fierceness and wrath of Almighty God.

16 And he hath on his vesture and on his thigh a name written, KING OF KINGS, AND LORD OF LORDS.

17 And I saw an angel standing in the sun; and he cried

with a loud voice, saying to all the fowls that fly in the midst of heaven, Come and gather yourselves together unto the supper of the great God.

The supper meal is a meal for the fowls of the air. This is the marriage supper of the Lamb and *the supper of the great God.* Christ taught His disciples about this in Luke 17:34-37: *I tell you, in that night there shall be two men in one bed; the one shall be taken, and the other shall be left. 35 Two women shall be grinding together; the one shall be taken, and the other left. 36 Two men shall be in the field; the one shall be taken, and the other left. 37 And they answered and said unto him, Where, Lord? And he said unto them, Wheresoever the body is, thither will the eagles be gathered together.* This is describing *the supper of the great God* which is *the marriage supper of the Lamb,* not the rapture of the church.

The Great Commission

In closing out this chapter, here are a few lingering thoughts about the NT, local church and God's will for its direction.   What makes our dispensation so drastically different than all the others, in the building of the kingdom, is the Incarnation (God [Jesus Christ] became flesh dwelt among us) and the Great Commission. Obedience to the Lord's command to go, to preach, and to teach all nations will be the measuring rod for every local church and its leadership. Any church's failure to equip the saints for the work of the ministry is a direct result of ignoring the third leg of the Great Commission, which is teaching. The goal of teaching is to impart knowledge. Knowledge is what one knows. If you know it, you can say it. You can say it because it's in your permanent memory. It's like counting to 100 or saying the a, b, c's.

The Scripture speaks of people being destroyed because of the lack of knowledge. Let's take a look here in Hosea 4:6: *My people are destroyed for lack of knowledge: because thou* [the leaders] *hast rejected knowledge, I will also reject thee, that thou shalt be no priest to me: seeing thou hast forgotten the law of thy God, I will also forget thy children.* God told the people to do something to prevent them from forgetting

His Word. He gave them these verses which instructed them to rehearse His Word until it was in their permanent memory. See it here in Deuteronomy 6:6-9: *6 And these words, which I command thee this day, shall be in thine heart: 7 And thou shalt teach them diligently unto thy children, and shalt talk of them when thou sittest in thine house, and when thou walkest by the way, and when thou liest down, and when thou risest up. 8 And thou shalt bind them for a sign upon thine hand, and they shall be as frontlets between thine eyes. 9 And thou shalt write them upon the posts of thy house, and on thy gates.* This is but one example of what God expected His people to do with His Word.

In the NT, there are similar commands to know God's Word. It is not only for the believer's spiritual strength, but to be able to give an answer to others. Here is an example of that in 1Peter 3:15: *But sanctify the Lord God in your hearts: and be ready always to give an answer to every man that asketh you a reason of the hope that is in you with meekness and fear.*

If you were only willing to work and labor over one

thing to get into your permanent memory, this would be worth it all. It's giving an answer to those who ask you about Jesus. The most unanswered question by Christians, at all levels, is the trinity question. Here are some aspects of the triunity of God and man that every Christian should have in his permanent memory. If you take the time and effort to learn them, you can teach them to your children, to your Sunday school class, and to people that ask you a reason of your hope.

I am praying that as you turn to the next page, you will learn more about Jesus and the awesome nature of our God. This knowledge will help prevent our generation and the generations to come from being destroyed.

The third leg (teaching and equipping the saints for the work of the ministry) of the Great Commission has been broken too long. It's time to set it straight again by creating learning centers in our churches. The goal of teaching is knowledge. Knowledge is what one knows. If you know it, you can say it. Can you explain the Trinity, Triunity, and Godhead?

Trinity

A word used to speak of the eternal relationship of the members of the Godhead—God the Father, God the Son, and God the Holy Spirit. The simplest expression of this truth is the answer to this question:

how can one explain the Trinity? It is the belief that God is one eternal being in three eternal persons. It can also be expressed in this manner: in the Godhead, there are three Persons. Each Person is fully God. There is only one God. What is the Godhead? The Godhead is a collective term that speaks of God the Father, God the Son, and God the Holy Spirit. Christ is said to be the fullness of the Godhead bodily, as expressed in Colossians 2:9: *"For in him [Jesus Christ] dwelleth all the fulness of the Godhead bodily."* The Bible supports the previous and following statement doctrinally.

The Father is called God (John 6:27). "Labour not for the meat which perisheth, but for that meat which endureth unto everlasting life, which the Son of man

198

shall give unto you: for him hath God the Father sealed."

Jesus is called God (John 1:1). "₁ₐ In the beginning was the Word, ₁ᵦ and the Word was with God, ₁ᵧ and the Word [title for Jesus] was God [a god is a false rendering of John ₁ᵧ and a contradiction to John 20:28 and many other verses]."

The Holy Spirit is called God (Acts 5:3-4). "But Peter said, Ananias, why hath Satan filled thine heart to lie to the Holy Ghost, and to keep back part of the price of the land?" 4 "Hast thou conceived this thing in thine heart? thou hast not lied unto men, but unto God."

There is only one God (1 Timothy 2:5). "For there is one God, and one mediator between God and men, the man Christ Jesus."

God created man in His image and likeness (Genesis 1:26-27). "And God said, Let us make man in our image, after our likeness: and let them have dominion over the fish of the sea, and over the fowl of the air, and over the cattle, and over all the earth, and over every creeping thing that creepeth upon the earth." 27 "So

God created man in his own image, in the image of God created he him; male and female created he them."

There is only one man (1 Thessalonians 5:23). "And the very God of peace sanctify you [the man or person] wholly; and I pray God your whole spirit and soul and body be preserved blameless unto the coming of our Lord Jesus Christ."

1. God is triune. He is one eternal being in three eternal persons.

2. God created man in His own image and likeness.

3. Man is triune. He is wholly man (not animal-like). There is only one man.

Observations

Why do we believe that the Father is God? Because the Bible calls Him God.

Why do we believe that the Son (Jesus Christ) is God? Because the Bible calls Him God.

Why do we believe that the Holy Spirit is God? Because the Bible calls Him God.

Why do we believe that there is only one God? Because the Bible declares that there is only one God.

Conclusion

Whereas the Bible calls the Father God, the Son God, and the Holy Spirit God and states that there is only one God, we must conclude that the Bible teaches that there is one Eternal God who is triune.

When the New Testament was completed, the mystery of the triunity of God was unveiled. God the Father sent His Son to be the sacrifice for all who would receive Him by faith. God the Son (Jesus Christ) became flesh and dwelt among us, and was crucified, buried, and resurrected on the third day after His death. He sent God the Holy Spirit to dwell in each child of God. What a blessing it is to believe these truths, and what an awesome God He is!

Lesson 2 Memorization

Question 1: What does the word "Trinity" mean?

Answer: It is a word used to speak of the eternal relationship of the members of the Godhead: God the Father, God the Son, and God the Holy Spirit.

Question 2: Why do we believe that the Father is God? Give the verse that states that the Father is God.

Answer: We believe that the Father is God because the Bible calls Him God (John 6:27).

Question 3: Why do we believe that Jesus is God? Give five verses that state that Jesus is God.

Answer: We believe that Jesus is God because the Bible calls Him God (Isaiah 9:6, John 1:1, John 20:28, 1 Timothy 3:16, Revelation 1:7-8).

Question 4: Why do we believe that the Holy Spirit is God? Give four verses that show this truth.

Answer: We believe that the Holy Spirit is God because the Bible calls Him God (Acts 5:3-4, 1 John 4:15, John 14:16-17, Romans 8:9).

Question 5: Could you explain the Trinity?

Answer: It is the belief that God is one eternal being in three eternal Persons. It can also be expressed in this manner: in the Godhead, there are three Persons. Each Person is fully God. There is only one God.

Question 6: What is the Godhead?

Answer: The Godhead is a word that speaks of God the Father, God the Son, and God the Holy Spirit. Christ is said to be the fullness of the Godhead bodily. As

Colossians 2:9 says, "For in him [Jesus Christ] dwelleth all the fulness of the Godhead bodily."

Question 7: What is the greatest evidence in creation that God is a triune being?

Answer: God's creation of man is the greatest evidence in creation that He is triune, for He created man in His own image and likeness. As Genesis 1:26-27 says: 26 "And God said, Let us make man in our image, after our likeness: and let them have dominion over the fish of the sea, and over the fowl of the air, and over the cattle, and over all the earth, and over every creeping thing that creepeth upon the earth." 27 "So God created man in his own image, in the image of God created he him; male and female created he them."

KINGDOM NATIONS

When I did my Berean search for nations, my Bible app listed 321 references. Probably the last reference in Revelation 22 strikes the greatest interest. It is a fitting conclusion to this chapter and is discussed in the last section of this study. If you read each of the verses written below, you will understand nations in context. When you read Revelation 21, it mentions nations and kings which bring their glory into the holy city, the new Jerusalem in Revelation 21:24-26: 24 *And the nations of them which are saved shall walk in the light of it: and the kings of the earth do bring their glory and honour into it. 25 And the gates of it shall not be shut at all by day: for there shall be no night there. 26 And they shall bring the glory and honour of the nations into it.* This sounds like the rewards given to the faithful servants of the pound and talents in Luke 19 and Matthew 25.

Daniel was given a revelation of the eternal kingdom and spoke of it in Daniel 7:14: *And there was given him* *dominion, and glory, and a kingdom, <u>that all people,</u> <u>nations</u>, and languages, should serve <u>him: his</u> <u>dominion is an everlasting dominion</u>, which shall not pass away, and his kingdom that which shall not be destroyed.*

Scripture makes it clear which nations will not survive the end time judgments. Here are a few examples that are notable:

Isa 60:12

For the nation and kingdom that will not serve thee shall perish; yea, those nations shall be utterly wasted.

Rev 11:18

And the nations were angry, and thy wrath is come, and the time of the dead, that they should be judged, and that thou shouldest give reward unto thy servants the prophets, and to the saints, and them that fear thy name, small and great; and shouldest destroy them which destroy the earth.

During the millennial reign of Christ, nations will develop; some will be good and some will be evil. The nations which enter into the eternal kingdom are referenced in these two passages:

Matt 25:31-34

31 When the Son of man shall come in his glory, and all the holy angels with him, then shall he sit upon the throne of his glory:

32 And before him shall be gathered all nations: and he shall separate them one from another, as a shepherd divideth his sheep from the goats [this takes place near the end of Christ's millennial reign]:

33 And he shall set the sheep on his right hand, but the goats on the left.

34 Then shall the King say unto them on his right hand, Come, ye blessed of my Father, inherit the kingdom prepared for you from the foundation of the world.

Now these verses in Revelation 20 describe this same event.

Rev 20:1-10

1 And I saw an angel come down from heaven, having the key of the bottomless pit and a great chain in his hand.

2 And he laid hold on the dragon, that old serpent,

which is the Devil, and Satan, and bound him a thousand years,

3 And cast him into the bottomless pit, and shut him up, and set a seal upon him, that he should deceive the nations no more, till the thousand years should be fulfilled: and after that he must be loosed a little season.

4 And I saw thrones, and they sat upon them, and judgment was given unto them: and I saw the souls of them that were beheaded for the witness of Jesus, and for the word of God, and which had not worshipped the beast, neither his image, neither had received his mark upon their foreheads, or in their hands; and they lived and reigned with Christ a thousand years.

5 But the rest of the dead lived not again until the thousand years were finished. This is the first resurrection.

6 Blessed and holy is he that hath part in the first resurrection: on such the second death hath no power, but they shall be priests of God and of Christ, and shall reign with him a thousand years.

7 And when the thousand years are expired, Satan shall

be loosed out of his prison,

8 And shall go out to deceive the nations which are in the four quarters of the earth, Gog and Magog, to gather them together to battle: the number of whom is as the sand of the sea.

9 And they went up on the breadth of the earth, and compassed the camp of the saints about, and the beloved city: and fire came down from God out of heaven, and devoured them.

10 And the devil that deceived them was cast into the lake of fire and brimstone, where the beast and the false prophet are [they are and will be forever], and shall be tormented day and night for ever and ever.

The nations left on this earth are the nations which will be in the new earth in Revelation 21. They are part of the nations that bring their glory into the new Jerusalem and worship the Lamb.

Nations in Revelation 22

Rev 22:1-5

1 And he shewed me a pure river of water of life, clear as crystal, proceeding out of the throne of God and of

the Lamb.

2 In the midst of the street of it, and on either side of the river, was there the tree of life, which bare twelve manner of fruits, and yielded her fruit every month: and the leaves of the tree were for the healing of the nations.

3 And there shall be no more curse: but the throne of God and of the Lamb shall be in it [the new Jerusalem]; and his servants shall serve him:

4 And they shall see his face; and his name shall be in their foreheads.

5 And there shall be no night there [in the new Jerusalem]; and they need no candle, neither light of the sun; for the Lord God giveth them light: and they [His chosen servants] shall reign for ever and ever.

The first question that could be asked from these five verses is whether these verses are connected to the millennial kingdom or the eternal kingdom in Revelation 21. Where do we find the answer to that question? We find it from the context of verses one and three. What is it, in these two verses, that establishes the link to Revelation 21? It's the word "throne." Take a look in Revelation 21:5: *And he [Jesus] that sat upon the throne said, Behold, I make all things new ....*

So, we know that the first five verses in Revelation 22 are linked to chapter 21. The next challenge is to understand the language in Revelation 22:1-2:

Rev 22:1-2

1 And he shewed me a pure <u>river of water of life</u>, clear as crystal, proceeding out of the throne of God and of the Lamb.

2 In the midst of the street of it, and on either side of the river, was there the <u>tree of life</u>, which bare <u>twelve manner of fruits</u>, and yielded her fruit every month: and the <u>leaves of the tree</u> were <u>for the healing of the nations</u>. The rules tell us that before something is figurative, it must be literal. With that in mind, let's start looking for water of life in a literal sense. When I searched for water of life with my Bible app, this verse was found in John 4:14: *But whosoever drinketh of the water that I shall give him shall never thirst; but <u>the water that I shall give</u> him shall be in him a well of <u>water springing</u>*

up into everlasting life. The language in this verse is figurative. So, we move on to the next verse that our search app referenced in Revelation 21:6: *And he* [Jesus] *said unto me, It is done. I am Alpha and Omega, the beginning and the end. I will give unto him that is athirst of the fountain of the water of life freely.* Still, we have no literal fountain of water that people can drink. The last two verses that the search referenced are the ones in Revelation 22:1,17: *1 And he shewed me a pure river of water of life, clear as crystal, proceeding out of the throne of God and of the Lamb. 17 And the Spirit and the bride say, Come. And let him that heareth say, Come. And let him that is athirst come. And whosoever will, let him take the water of life freely.*

Verse 17 is connected in thought to this passage in John 7:37-39: *In the last day, that great day of the feast, Jesus stood and cried, saying, If any man thirst, let him come unto me, and drink. 38 He that believeth on me, as the scripture hath said, out of his belly shall flow rivers of living water. 39 (But this spake he of the Spirit,*

which they that believe on him should receive: for the
Holy Ghost was not yet given; because that Jesus was
not yet glorified.)

Now, after reviewing what our Scripture search has revealed, we know that the figurative language for *water of life* was a symbol for the Holy Spirit.

This leaves Revelation 22:1 to stand alone as a verse in which the context is literal rather than figurative. What do you mean by that? Well, let's look again at verse one.

Rev 22:1

And he shewed me a pure river of water of life, clear as crystal, proceeding out of the throne of God and of the Lamb.

And he shewed me: What John was looking at, was literal. It was a river. The throne that he saw, was literal. It is said that John saw and heard these things in Revelation 22:8: *And I John saw these things, and heard them. And when I had heard and seen, I fell down to worship before the feet of the angel which shewed me these things.* We may therefore, understand that the things which John saw were literal.

Nations Healing

Now, let's take a look at Revelation 22:2 and examine it the same way. This is the verse that speaks about the healing of the nations.

Rev 22:2

In the midst of the street of it, and on either side of the river, was there <u>the tree of life</u>, which bare twelve manner of <u>fruits</u>, and yielded her fruit every month: and the <u>leaves</u> of the tree <u>were for the healing of the nations</u>. Remembering the rules that something has to be literal before it can be figurative, we can ask this question, "Was there ever a literal tree of life?" The answer is yes, and it is recorded in Genesis 2:9: *And out of the ground made the LORD God to grow every tree that is pleasant to the sight, and good for food; <u>the tree of life also in the midst of the garden</u>, and the tree of knowledge of good and evil.*

The next thought that comes to mind is what nations are spoken of and why would they need to be healed? The only nations left in Revelation 20 are those that did not rebel and follow Satan. These nations are, in a moment of time, on the new earth. If this is a factor in their need of healing, it is not mentioned. The Scripture gives no details, in the context of verse two, that would answer our question about fruit and leaves.

The next question generated is how do the leaves of the tree of life heal the nations? Again, there is nothing in the context that answers that question. Unanswered questions, in situations like this, are more beneficial than questions that are answered incorrectly.

Just when I thought my pen was about to rest with this subject, I decided to search for one more word from the Revelation 22 verses. The word that seems to have been illuminated and begging for attention was **foreheads**. So, I started looking for other references. Well, praise the Lord, I am so thankful for the nudge. You will see an incredible match of words and context that are in Revelation 7:1-17. To see the connection, I will place the matching verses in parallel.

Rev 22:1-4

1 And he shewed me a pure river of water of life, clear

as crystal, proceeding out of the throne of God and of the Lamb.

2 In the midst of the street of it, and on either side of the river, was there the tree of life, which bare twelve manner of fruits, and yielded her fruit every month: and the leaves of the tree were for the healing of the nations.

3 And there shall be no more curse: but the throne of God and of the Lamb shall be in it; and his servants shall serve him:

4 And they shall see his face; and his name shall be in their **foreheads**.

If a picture is truly worth a 1000 words, then what you are about to see should help tremendously. The word search for foreheads has provided helpful context and harmony that was previously lacking. Believing that Scripture is the Bible's most reliable commentary, is what compels one to follow the Berean search principle.

These verses connect the dots and answer the question about the occupants of the holy city. Take a look at how a "Berean search" truly brings context together.

THE NEW JERUSALEM — THE HOLY CITY
WHO ARE ITS OCCUPANTS?

Rev 7:3-4;13-17

3 Saying, Hurt not the earth, neither the sea, nor the trees, till we have sealed the servants of our God in their **foreheads**.

4 And I heard the number of them which were sealed: and there were sealed an hundred and forty and four thousand of all the tribes of the children of Israel.

13And one of the elders answered, saying unto me, What are these which are arrayed in white robes? and whence came they?

14 And I said unto him, Sir, thou knowest. And he said to me, These are they which came out of great tribulation, and have washed their robes, and made them white in the blood of the Lamb.

15 Therefore are they before the throne of God, and serve him day and night in his temple: and he that sitteth on the throne shall dwell among them.

16 They shall hunger no more, neither thirst any more; neither shall the sun light on them, nor any heat.

17 For the Lamb which is in the midst of the throne shall feed them, and shall lead them unto living fountains of waters: and God shall wipe away all tears from their eyes.

Rev 14:1-5

1 And I looked, and, lo, a Lamb stood on the mount Sion, and with him an hundred forty and four thousand, having his Father's name written in their **foreheads**.

2 And I heard a voice from heaven, as the voice of many waters, and as the voice of a great thunder: and I heard the voice of harpers harping with their harps:

3 And they sung as it were a new song before the throne, and before the four beasts, and the elders: and no man could learn that song but the hundred and forty and four thousand, which were redeemed from the earth.

4 These are they which were not defiled with women; for they are virgins. These are they which follow the Lamb whithersoever he goeth. These were redeemed from among men, being the firstfruits unto God and to the Lamb.

5 And in their mouth was found no guile: for they are without fault before the throne of God.

Rev 22:1-5

1 And he shewed me a pure river of water of life, clear as crystal, proceeding out of the throne of God and of the Lamb.

2 In the midst of the street of it, and on either side of the river, was there the tree of life, which bare twelve manner of fruits, and yielded her fruit every month: and the leaves of the tree were for the healing of the nations.

3 And there shall be no more curse: but the throne of God and of the Lamb shall be in it; and his servants shall serve him:

4 And they [His servants] shall see his face; and his name shall be in their **foreheads**.

5 And there shall be no night there; and they need no candle, neither light of the sun; for the Lord God giveth them light: and they [His servants] shall reign for ever and ever.

The Lord told His disciples that those who would suffer for Him, would also reign with Him. They will be in the holy city serving Him for time without end. What an honor these servants have been given. Blessed is the Lord who honors them who honor Him. Amen!

This brings our kingdom nations thoughts to a close. We trust that it would have been a help and blessing to each reader. A special thanks to the one reading this now, who asked me the questions that brought these final thoughts to my attention.

May God bless you all and enjoy the kingdom!

The Berean Principle

Acts 17:11
"... they received the word with all <u>readiness</u> of mind, and searched the scriptures daily, whether those things were so."
© BWCE

KINGDOM TREE

As our kingdom words were about to reach their end, one lingering thought emerged from the keyboard. It was beckoning for one final search and a little space at the end of our journey. Well, how could I say no? That final search was for *the tree of life*.

Did you ever wonder what happened to the tree of life that was in the Garden of Eden? Remember when the Lord drove Adam and Eve from the garden, He placed Cherubims with a flaming sword to protect it. Why did God do that? Our Creator did that because it was a real tree of life. Anyone who would partake of it, would live forever in a new earth with access to the holy city. Well, our search found that tree. The Lord saved the best for the very last words of His message. Take a look at the tree that gives everlasting life!

Rev 2:7

He that hath an ear, let him hear what the Spirit saith unto the churches; To him that overcometh will I give to eat of the tree of life ….

Rev 22:2

In the midst of the street of it [the holy city], and on either side of the river, was there the tree of life ....

Rev 22:14

Blessed are they that do his commandments, that they may have right to the tree of life, and may enter in through the gates into the city.

If you have been searching for the tree of life, it's there. Take God at His Word and you will be able to eat of its fruit. Being a church member, you may read about it. Being on the choir, you may sing about it. Being a teacher, you may teach about it. But to have the right to eat of it, you must be an overcomer (look again at Rev 2:7). Faith is the victory that overcomes the world. Genuine faith results in a new birth — becoming a child of God. God's children will have the right to partake of the tree of life. His children have access to the tree of life in the new Jerusalem, the city of God. Are you an overcomer? If not, surrender your life to Jesus Christ now and be willing to obey and serve Him.

KINGDOM LOVE

I read something recently that started me thinking about the Apostles and their love for Jesus. Well, really, how differently people responded to Jesus with love. It started with reading the verses where Jesus chose His first four disciples. They were two sets of brothers who were fishing buddies. Simon, called Peter, and Andrew, and then straightway He called James and John. All four of them immediately left nets and followed the Master. Their lives would forever be changed. Jesus planned to make them fishers of men. Little did they know, at that time, that their names would be eternally etched in the foundations of the holy city, the new Jerusalem, as recorded in Rev 21:14: *And the wall of the city had twelve foundations, and in them the names of the twelve apostles of the Lamb.*

Peter, James, and his brother, John, were those of Christ's inner circle. James was the first to be martyred. The account of his death is found in Acts 12:1-2: *Now about that time Herod the king stretched forth his hands to vex certain of the church. 2 And he killed James the brother of John with the sword.* So, James was the first to drink the cup of death that Jesus spoke of in Matthew 20:20-22: *20 Then came to him the mother of Zebedee's children with her sons, worshipping him, and desiring a certain thing of him. 21 And he said unto her, What wilt thou? She saith unto him, Grant that these my two sons may sit, the one on thy right hand, and the other on the left, in thy kingdom. 22 But Jesus answered and said, Ye know not what ye ask. Are ye able to drink of the cup that I shall drink of, and to be baptized with the baptism that I am baptized with? They say unto him, We are able.*

It has often been said that all the Apostles died a martyr's death, with the exception of John, Andrew's brother. There is great love in dying and there is also great love in living. John had the ladder. David was a man after God's own heart, but John was a man who felt it beat because of his great love. You can sense that in John 13:23: *Now there was leaning on Jesus' bosom one of his disciples, whom Jesus loved.* And that disciple was John. Have you ever had the desire to do what John did? For all those of you who have, He knows your heart. Keep on longing for that moment, and maybe, one day the Lord will give you the desires of your heart also.

Did you ever wonder why it is said that Jesus loved Mary, Martha, and Lazarus? The story is so touching and overflowing with passion. The kind of passion that makes one want to be at the table with them the next time He's there. His relationship with these three siblings seems to be exceptional. How did they ever get so close to the Savior? This is God who lovingly comes to their rescue, who weeps with compassion for their sorrow. How can that happen to anyone? Don't you want to know? It's got to be written down somewhere, right? And it is in Proverbs 8:17: *I love them that love me; and those that seek me early shall find me.* Now, the me in this verse is wisdom, but it is a fitting application to God in John 16:27: *For the Father himself loveth you, because ye have loved me, and have believed that I came out from God.*

Kingdom love is something that's now, not when you get to glory. What is love? Someone said that it is a selfless concern and care for others. Well, how does one get like that? When one's desire to be more like Jesus is real, so real, that you become a little less self-centered, bit by bit, that's a start. It is certain that what one does now will have kingdom effects.

God equates a major part of love as obedience. How many times did Jesus say that if you love Me, keep My commandments? Loving obedience is a part of what gives love a chance to grow. When love grows, the heart glows. When the heart glows, people will know that your words and actions are genuine. Can you give me some examples that fit this context? Well, how about this in Matthew 5:44-45: *But I say unto you, Love your enemies, bless them that curse you, do good to them that hate you, and pray for them which despitefully use you, and persecute you; 45 That ye may be the children of your Father which is in heaven.* When you are around Mary, Martha, Lazarus, and John in the Scriptures, do you get the feeling they're responding with this kind of love?

If your life were to end right now, and your kingdom position would be determined by your love habits, for lack of a better word, would you be satisfied? I must say, "Oh, Lord, help me, I have a long way to go to make the entry level on the love scale. Please help me to grow!"

Kingdom love is something that we long for and cannot imagine how wonderful it will feel to love and be loved like Jesus. We will be like Him the Scripture says. We will be in a new world with pure hearts that will never feel the effects of sin again. The kingdom is the love of God freely given to those who have come to His Son for forgiveness and a new life.

Thank you for allowing me to share these kingdom thoughts with each of you. We have so much to be thankful for and so much to look forward to in heaven and beyond. God bless you and keep the love of Christ flowing in your hearts until you see Him face to face.

Our Father in heaven, Hallowed be Thy name. Thy kingdom come. Thy will be done until our race is run.

302597R00124

Made in the USA
Columbia, SC
01 March 2019